Accounts and Audit of Limited Liability Partnerships

Second edition

Yvonne Lang BSc, FCA
Clare Copeman BA, ACA

Tottel
publishing

Tottel Publishing Ltd, Maxwelton House, 41–43 Boltro Road, Haywards Heath, West Sussex, RH16 1BJ

A CIP Catalogue record for this book is available from the British Library.

ISBN 13   978 1 84592 810 0

Typeset, printed and bound in Great Britain by M & A Thomson Litho Ltd, East Kilbride, Scotland

Preface to the Second Edition

Since the legislation allowing the formation of Limited Liability Partnerships (LLPs) came into effect in April 2001, some 25,000 businesses have been set up as LLPs. While a large proportion of these have been professional practices previously operating as general partnerships, the flexibility offered by the LLP structure has made them attractive for operations in many different industries.

The detailed accounting requirements are set out in the Limited Liability Partnerships Regulations 2001 which broadly mirror the requirements of legislation applicable to limited companies including the need to follow accounting standards.

The application of accounting standards to some aspects of the way in which LLPs are structured led the Consultative Committee of Accounting Bodies (CCAB) to commission a Working Party to develop a Statement of Recommended Practice (SORP) to cover the Accounting for Limited Liability Partnerships with the first version being issued in May 2002.

Since 2002, there have been a number of major changes in UK accounting standards primarily driven by the process of convergence with International Financial Reporting Standards. Of these changes by far the most significant was the adoption of new standards dealing with accounting for financial instruments. The ramifications of these new standards have been significant for many entities and the need for specific guidance for LLPs resulted in the CCAB asking the Working Party to revise the SORP and a new version was issued in March 2006. The process of revising the SORP was used both as an opportunity to provide much needed guidance on new standards and also to refine other aspects of the previous SORP to reflect practical experience over the three years since LLPs first came into existence.

In this second edition we have also been able to reflect on some of the practical issues that are faced by LLPs and their auditors as well as give full consideration to the pertinent accounting and auditing issues. In addition to thanking Clare Copeman, one of my fellow directors at Smith & Williamson, who wrote the chapters dealing with members' interests and revenue recognition, I would like to thank Colin Ives, a director in our Professional Practices Team, for the chapter on taxation and William Wastie and Jon Cheney from Addleshaw Goddard for the chapter on the legal aspects of LLPs.

Preface

I hope that this book will provide a useful reference for all those who work in and advise LLPs.

Yvonne Lang
National Technical Director
Smith & Williamson

Contents

Abbreviations and Definitions

ASB	=	Accounting Standards Board
CA 85	=	Companies Act 1985
CA 06	=	Companies Act 2006
CCAB	=	Consultative Committee of Accountancy Bodies
EEA	=	European Economic Area
EU	=	European Union
FRS	=	Financial Reporting Standard (issued by the ASB)
FRSSE	=	Financial Reporting Standard for Smaller Entities
HMRC	=	HM Revenue & Customs
IFRS	=	International Financial Reporting Standard
LLP	=	Limited Liability Partnership
LLPA	=	Limited Liability Partnerships Act 2000
LLP 2001 or 'the Regulations'	=	Limited Liability Partnerships Regulations 2001, SI 2001/1090
SORP	=	Statement of Recommended Practice *Accounting by Limited Liability Partnerships*
SSAP	=	Statement of Standard Accounting Practice (issued by the predecessor body to the ASB)
STRGL	=	Statement of total recognised gains and losses
UITF	=	Urgent Issues Task Force (assists the ASB in providing guidance on specific accounting areas; produces UITF Abstracts)

Chapter 1

The law and practice of limited liability partnerships

1 INTRODUCTION

1.1 The Limited Liability Partnerships Act 2000 (LLPA) created the first new major form of legal vehicle available under UK law since the establishment of joint stock companies in 1844. The law came into force on 6 April 2001 and by the beginning of 2007 over 25,000 businesses had registered as LLPs. LLPs were introduced in Northern Ireland in November 2004, with the Limited Liability Partnerships Regulations (Northern Ireland) 2004 implementing the Limited Liability Partnerships Act (Northern Ireland) 2002. The most important feature of the LLP is that it is an independent legal entity. It is a body corporate and not a partnership. An LLP, however, provides the benefits of a partnership in that members (they are referred to as 'members' and not 'partners' in the legislation) are free to organise their own internal affairs through a private members' agreement, and crucially the LLP's profits are taxed in the same way as a partnership, in the hands of its members and not the entity itself. However, unlike a partnership, an LLP has separate legal personality and unlimited capacity to contract. Members are the agents of the LLP and not of each other. The concept of mutual agency between partners, which results in innocent partners being bound by the acts of fellow partners to the full extent of their personal assets, does not apply to LLPs.

The limitation of members' personal liability will be central to those considering either setting up or transferring their business to an LLP. Its limitations should, however, also be understood. Although a member's personal assets should be protected in the event of a catastrophic or 'Armageddon' claim against the LLP to the extent it exceeds the firm's professional indemnity insurance cover and assets, there will still be the need to adopt strict risk management procedures. Professional practices should maintain their indemnity insurance levels and all members will continue (in much the same way as directors in companies) to be personally liable for their own negligent acts and defaults where they have assumed a personal responsibility to a client which has subsequently been relied upon. Where the LLP has client relationships and where it is permitted, terms of engagement should seek to limit personal liability. This is, however, a complex area and legal advice should always be sought.

As a consequence of what was referred to in the House of Lords' debates during the passage of the LLP legislation, as the 'great privilege' of limited liability status, an LLP is required to file audited accounts. Most of the provisions of the Companies Acts in respect of the preparation and filing of accounts are therefore applied to LLPs (see Chapter 2). An LLP can, as a body corporate, also grant charges over its undertakings. In addition, most of the provisions of the Insolvency Act 1986 are also applicable to an LLP.

2 THE LEGISLATION

1.2 The LLPA is a short Act of 19 sections, the longest of which concern taxation and ensuring that the position in respect of LLPs and taxation is the same as for general law partnerships, as well as providing that there is (subject to various conditions being met) tax neutrality on the transfer of a partnership's business to an LLP.

However, the LLPA cannot be read in isolation from the Limited Liability Partnerships Regulations 2001 (the Regulations). Parts II to IV make applicable to LLPs the relevant parts of the Companies Act 1985 (CA 85), the Company Directors Disqualification Act 1986, and the Insolvency Act 1986. These have to be read together with the Schedules to the Regulations which set out the modifications to the relevant statutes. Publications are available which incorporate these modifications into the actual body of the legislation, which makes it much easier to understand the necessary detail.

Part V of the Regulations applies provisions of the Financial Services and Markets Act 2000 to LLPs. Part VI sets out a set of default rules which will apply to an LLP in the absence of a members' agreement. For the reasons set out later in this chapter those forming an LLP would generally be ill-advised to allow themselves to be governed by these default rules.

The full extent of the impact of the new Companies Act 2006 (CA 06) on the LLP legislation is not clear at the time of publication. The bulk of the Act is unlikely to come into force until 2008 and we are still awaiting the new LLP Regulations which will cross refer to the provisions of CA 06.

3 INCORPORATION

1.3 As a result of its corporate status the incorporation of an LLP follows much the same procedure as the incorporation of a company. The

LLPA states that before an LLP can be incorporated 'two or more persons associated for carrying on a lawful business with a view to profit' must have subscribed their names to an incorporation document. This is a wider definition than under the Partnership Act 1890, s 1 which defines the relationship between partners as one of 'persons carrying on business in common with a view of profit'. 'Persons' includes not only individuals but also corporate entities such as another LLP or company. LLPs are not limited to regulated professions as had originally been the government's intention and their uses can be extremely varied and are only likely to be prohibited by illegality.

An LLP also has no share capital or memorandum and articles of association. There is no equivalent to Table A of CA 85 in respect of the internal relationships between members.

4 FORMING AN LLP

1.4 To incorporate an LLP, Form LLP2 has to be completed and delivered to Companies House with a registration fee (currently £20, or £50 for a 'same day' incorporation). The forms can be obtained from the Companies House website at www.companies-house.gov.uk and various guidance notes are available. Form LLP2 requires the name of the LLP which is to be registered, the names and addresses of the members and specification of which members are to be designated members. The duties and obligations of the designated members, which are much like those of a company secretary, are dealt with later in this chapter.

An LLP cannot have the same name as a registered company or another LLP. It is, however, inadvisable to use a shelf LLP to protect a name in the way in which shelf companies are used. This is because the stamp duty and stamp duty land tax rules on the transfer of business to an LLP (LLPA, s 12 and Finance Act 2003, s 65) provide an exemption from stamp duty where there is identical membership in the predecessor partnership immediately prior to incorporation and in the LLP after incorporation. The exemption is, however, only available for a period of 12 months from the date of incorporation.

The appropriate route for name protection continues to be the use of a shelf company. Section 723B of CA 85 makes provision for maintaining the confidentiality of a member's home address. To obtain such an order, a member of an LLP must show that there is a serious risk that they or a person living with them may be subject to violence or intimidation. There is a fee of £100 and any order by the Secretary of State will remain in force for five years and is renewable. It should be noted that these provisions are not retrospective and therefore once an address is on the register it will not be expunged from the existing records. It is worth noting that CA 06 will remove the requirement for directors of companies to file a residential address and they will, instead, only be required to file a service address. It is understood that this will apply equally to members of LLPs.

Form LLP2 also carries a formal statement of compliance, to be completed either by a member or the solicitor engaged in the formation of the LLP to the effect that the persons named on the form as members are associated for carrying on a lawful business with a view to profit. The nature of the business does not have to be stated.

The Registrar of Companies will issue a certificate of incorporation of the LLP with its own registered number which begins with the prefix OC3. The detailed rules in respect of the display of a registered company's name and details on business stationery and at its premises apply to LLPs and as a consequence it will be important to register the LLP well in advance of the actual transfer of the business to an LLP so that the necessary details are available for the LLP's stationery and signage. The recent amendments to ss 349 and 351 of CA 85 have extended the disclosure formalities for LLPs and companies, and now require statutory formalities to be displayed on websites.

Where any new member is appointed to the LLP, Form LLP288a providing that member's details has to be submitted to Companies House within 14 days of his appointment. The same applies for the termination of the appointment of a member, the relevant form being LLP288b.

5 THE MEMBERS' AGREEMENT

1.5 The default rules set out in the Regulations are unlikely to be suitable for the majority of LLPs. They draw heavily on the Partnership Act 1890, although the LLPA specifically disapplies partnership law to LLPs. The default rules provide, for example, that each member is entitled to share equally in the capital and profits of the LLP, that every member can take part in the management of the LLP and that the consent of all existing members is necessary before a new member can be admitted. In addition, differences between members concerning ordinary matters connected with the business may be decided by a majority of the members.

For a business of any size or sophistication these rules will be inappropriate and incapable of providing a workable management structure. Furthermore, the legislation clearly contemplates LLPs regulating their own internal structure and management and there are various central issues (for example, the application to LLPs of CA 85, s 459 regarding the protection of minorities from unfairly prejudicial conduct) which are not addressed in the default rules.

The members' agreement is a private document and does not have to be filed at Companies House. As well as dealing with the usual matters found in a partnership agreement such as management structure, sharing of profits (and losses), admission of members, contribution of capital, the conduct of members and their departure there are issues unique to LLPs that must be addressed.

These include the powers and duties of the designated members, the preparation, approval and audit of the statutory accounts, the ability and authority to create fixed and floating charges and the position of any salaried members. One other major issue is the effect of the company insolvency regime being applicable to LLPs. The members' agreement must deal with the effect of a dissolution, either by acts of the members or by virtue of insolvency. Furthermore, unlike in a partnership, it is possible to have a members' voluntary liquidation of an LLP and the powers of reconstruction set out in the Insolvency Act 1986 apply to LLPs. The legal opinion set out in Appendix 1 of the first LLP SORP (and repeated in Appendix 4 of the second SORP) in respect of the difference between distribution and allocation of profits (see Chapter 5) means that the profit-sharing mechanism will need to be carefully worded. Whilst the second LLP SORP classifies amounts owing to members as either debt or equity, the general principles regarding the distinction between the allocation and division of profits remain unchanged.

Whilst a partnership agreement will often provide the basic structure for a members' agreement the new, often corporate concepts are technical and it is fundamentally important to have them correctly drafted. The drawing up of the members' agreement is not a job for the amateur and the expense of getting it right will stand any LLP in good stead for its commercial future. It will also provide an opportunity for existing partnerships to conduct an extensive review of their current internal arrangements.

6 DESIGNATED MEMBERS

1.6 LLPs have to have at least two designated members who have a number of defined responsibilities and duties. On incorporation the LLP will have to state whether all the members are to be designated or name those who are. This position can be subsequently changed. Companies House must be notified of any changes to the designated members (Form LLP288c) within 14 days. Designated members automatically cease to be designated when they cease to be members. In larger organisations there will probably be a small group of designated members (ie those who are involved in management and compliance issues) whilst in the smaller organisation it may be that each member should assume the role.

The key duties of designated members include the signing (on behalf of members) and filing of the annual accounts, the appointment of the auditors and determining their remuneration, making a statutory declaration of solvency on a members' voluntary winding up and filing the various statutory returns (for example, the LLP's annual return and the notification to the Registrar of a change in membership in the LLP). There are penalties for breaches of the filing requirements in the form of fines. In most cases the legislation provides protection for designated members who were not knowingly and wilfully involved in the offence in question or where they took reasonable steps to avoid an offence occurring.

7 DUTIES AND RESPONSIBILITIES OF MEMBERS

1.7 The relationship between members should be regulated by the members' agreement. As already explained by virtue of LLPA, s 6(1) each member is the agent of the LLP and not of each other. This is the basis for the protection of members from personal liability in respect of another member's negligence.

Section 6 further provides that an LLP is not bound by anything done by a member dealing with another person if that member has no authority for that act and that person either knows the member has no authority or does not know or believe the member to be a member of the LLP.

Where a member is liable to a third party (other than another member) as a result of his own wrongful act or omission in the course of the business, then the LLP will be liable to that person to the same extent as the member. The possibility of a member still being liable for his own wrongful acts and omissions is discussed above. Such remaining personal liability may possibly be excluded by clear terms of engagement between the LLP and its clients and again this is an area where those considering converting to LLP status would be well advised to take professional advice.

Chapter 2

General accounting requirements and the LLP SORP

1 STATUTORY PROVISIONS

2.1 The original accounting requirements for LLPs are set out in LLPR 2001, reg 3 and Sch 1. These provisions take CA 85, Pt VII (accounts and audit) which deals with the requirements to prepare accounts, together with the relevant Schedules (4, 4A, 5, 7, 8, 8A and 10A) of that Act, which detail the content of those accounts, and make such modifications as are necessary to deal with the particular circumstances of LLPs.

Subsequent changes to CA 85 have been reflected in legislation applicable to LLPs by way of Statutory Instrument. As a consequence LLPs have either been required to comply with the changes or, in a number of cases, amendments have been disapplied. Some of the most notable recent changes in CA 85 have increased the disclosures required within the directors' reports of companies but many of these do not apply to LLPs, including the requirements for an enhanced business review.

2 THE IMPACT OF THE COMPANIES ACT 2006

2.2 The Companies Act 2006 received Royal Assent in November 2006, although the majority of its provisions will not come into force until late 2007 or 2008. In due course the legislation applicable to LLPs will need to be rewritten to reflect CA 06, and to the extent it is possible to anticipate the effect on LLPs, potential legislative changes have been reflected throughout this book.

3 REQUIREMENTS TO KEEP ACCOUNTING RECORDS

2.3 The level of sophistication of the accounting records maintained by an LLP will vary dependent on its size and the complexity of the business it undertakes. The minimum requirements are that the accounting records must be sufficient to record and explain the LLP's transactions and disclose with reasonable accuracy, at any time, the financial position of the LLP. They must also contain sufficient information to enable accounts to be prepared in accordance with the legislation. Failure to maintain adequate records is an offence and is a matter which is required to be referred to in the audit report (see **3.6**).

The accounting records are required to be kept at the registered office unless the members consider it appropriate to keep them elsewhere. The members of the LLP have the right to inspect the records at any time. To the extent that the records are held outside the United Kingdom, accounts and returns with respect to those records must be sent to, and retained in, the United Kingdom.

Whilst the legislation requires that accounting records be retained for three years from the date on which they are prepared, tax legislation requires that the records be retained for five years and ten months from the end of the tax year in which the accounting period ends. For example, records relating to accounts prepared for the year ended 30 April 2006 would need to be retained until 31 January 2013. There may also be other requirements specific to the nature of the business of the LLP (for example where it has long-term contracts) which would result in a longer period of retention being necessary.

4 ACCOUNTING REFERENCE DATES AND ACCOUNTING PERIODS

2.4 For the first period after incorporation the accounting reference date of an LLP (ie the date to which the accounts are prepared) is the last day of the month in which the anniversary of its incorporation falls. In the absence of any application to shorten or lengthen the accounting period (see below), the first accounting period will start on the date of incorporation and end on that accounting reference date. The first accounting period cannot be longer than 18 months. Subsequent accounting periods will then cover a year from the date of the end of the previous accounting period unless an application is made to amend the accounting reference date.

To make provision for those LLPs who want to prepare their accounts for a 52 (or 53) week period, accounts may be prepared to a date which is no more than seven days either side of the accounting reference date.

Where an LLP has subsidiary undertakings, the members should ensure that the financial year of each subsidiary coincides with that of the LLP, unless there is a good reason for it not to. For example, where the regulations of an overseas jurisdiction require a different date.

LLPs are able to change their accounting reference dates, subject to certain rules. It is possible to change:

- for the current accounting reference period (and subsequent periods); or
- when the accounting reference date has already passed, for the immediately preceding accounting reference period, provided that the period for filing accounts (see **2.8**) has not expired.

An LLP cannot usually extend its accounting period more than once in any five-year period. The exception is where the LLP becomes a subsidiary or parent and the change is necessary in order to align accounting reference dates across a group.

5 FORM AND CONTENT OF ACCOUNTS

2.5 The members are responsible for preparing at the end of each financial year a profit and loss account and balance sheet which give a true and fair view of the state of affairs of the LLP at the end of the financial period and of the profit or loss for that financial period. A report to the members (members' report) is also required. The form and content of the balance sheet, profit and loss account and notes to the accounts are currently set out in Schedule 4 to CA 85 (as amended).

The fact that the accounts of an LLP are required to give a true and fair view means that they also have to comply with all extant SSAPs, FRSs and UITF Abstracts. Therefore, where required, they will also need to include a cash flow statement and statement of total recognised gains and losses (STRGL).

As discussed in more detail in Chapter 5, the SORP also requires disclosure of total members' interests on the face of the balance sheet, as a memorandum item.

An illustrative set of accounts for an LLP is set out in Appendix 1.

6 STATEMENT OF RECOMMENDED PRACTICE – ACCOUNTING BY LIMITED LIABILITY PARTNERSHIPS

2.6 The most recent version of the SORP was issued by the CCAB (the six major accountancy institutes in UK and Ireland) in March 2006 and has been subject to limited review by the ASB, whose key role was to ensure that it did not include anything that conflicted with existing accounting standards. Development of the SORP is overseen by a steering committee whose membership is drawn from trades and professions whose members are, or are expected to become, LLPs.

Whilst there is no legal requirement to comply with the SORP, non-compliance would need to be reported in the accounts and it is likely that the non-compliance would result in the accounts not giving a true and fair view, resulting in qualification of the audit report.

The SORP does not provide details of all of the reporting requirements which are applicable to LLPs, but it does provide interpretation of those accounting standards where there are specific issues regarding their application to the circumstances of an LLP. There is a requirement within the SORP that the note to the financial statements which deals with accounting policies should refer to the LLP's compliance with the SORP, together with any non-compliance and the reasons.

Areas dealt with within the SORP are as follows:

- The contents of the annual report and financial statements.
- Members' remuneration and interests.
- Retirement benefits.
- Taxation.
- Revenue recognition – stocks and long-term contracts.
- Business combinations and group accounts.
- Provisions and other implications of FRS 12.
- Related parties.

7 GROUPS

2.7 Where, at the end of the financial period, an LLP is a parent undertaking both individual and group (consolidated) accounts are required. The LLP is not required to present its own profit and loss account as part of those group accounts, but must state that it has taken advantage of the exemption contained in CA 85, s 230 (as amended). The profit and loss account is, however, still required to be prepared and approved by the members.

Exemption from the preparation of group accounts is available where the LLP is itself a wholly or majority (greater than 50 per cent) owned subsidiary. The exemption is conditional on the following:

- The LLP must be included in consolidated accounts prepared by the parent of a larger group and those accounts are either at the same date as the LLP's own accounts or an earlier date in the same financial year.
- Where the parent is established under the law of an EEA State, the accounts of the parent must be prepared either in accordance with the provisions of the Seventh Directive 83/349/EEC or international financial reporting standards.
- Where the parent is not established under the law of an EEA State the accounts of the parent must be prepared either in accordance with the Seventh Directive or an 'equivalent manner'. Guidance on the interpretation of equivalence has been issued by the Urgent Issues Task Force in Abstract 43 'The interpretation of equivalence for the purposes of section 228A of The Companies Act 1985'.
- The parent company accounts must be audited.
- The LLP must disclose that it is exempt from the requirement to prepare group accounts together with the name of the parent within whose accounts the LLP is included.
- Copies of the parent's group accounts have to be filed with the Registrar of Companies. If they are not in English, a certified translation must be attached.

Subsidiaries may be excluded from consolidation in the following circumstances:

- The amounts are immaterial and also immaterial in aggregate.
- Severe long-term restrictions exist which hinder the LLP from exercising its rights over the subsidiary.
- Control by the LLP is only temporary.

8 APPROVAL, PUBLICATION AND FILING OF ACCOUNTS

2.8 The accounts are required to be approved by the members and signed on their behalf by a designated member. Obtaining the approval of all members can pose potential practical problems because of the large numbers that could be involved. However, use of electronic communication (email, websites, intranets, etc) should considerably simplify the process.

A copy of the accounts together with the audit report (see Chapter 3) is required to be sent to every member within one month of approval. Advantage can be taken of the Companies Act 1985 (Electronic Communications) Order 2000, SI 2000/3373 which also applies to LLPs. The order permits accounts to be distributed electronically to any member so long as their prior approval has been obtained. Where this provision is to be used by the LLP, it can either agree with individual members that the accounts will be sent by email to them or that the accounts will be published on a website and the member will be notified as to where the accounts can be viewed. These provisions are likely to be particularly advantageous to LLPs as frequently the majority of members have access to the same computer systems and information sources within the organisation.

The designated members are responsible for delivering the accounts to the Registrar of Companies—in practice this will most probably be delegated to one person. Delivery to the Registrar currently has to be within ten months of the period end, although applying the requirements of CA06 to LLPs will reduce this to nine months. Where it is the first accounting period and it covers more than 12 months, the period allowed is ten months from the anniversary of the date of incorporation or three months from the end of the accounting reference period, whichever expires last.

9 SPECIAL PROVISIONS APPLICABLE TO SMALL AND MEDIUM-SIZED LLPS

2.9 Qualification as a small or medium-sized LLP is based on the requirements in CA 85. The qualifying conditions, of which two or more have to be met, are as follows:

	Small LLP
Turnover	Not more than £5.6 million
Balance sheet total	Not more than £2.8 million
Number of employees	Not more than 50
	Medium-sized LLP
Turnover	Not more than £22.8 million
Balance sheet total	Not more than £11.4 million
Number of employees	Not more than 250

An LLP qualifies as small or medium-sized in the following circumstances:

- If in respect of the first financial period it meets the criteria for that period.

- For subsequent financial years it meets the criteria in both that year and the previous year.
- It met the qualifying criteria in the preceding year.

The provisions do not apply if the LLP was at any time within the financial period authorised to undertake insurance business, an e-money issuer, an ISD investment firm or a UCITS management company or it was a member of an ineligible group. An ineligible group is one where any of its members is a public company or body corporate whose shares are admitted to trading in an EEA state, a banking company, an authorised insurance business, an e-money issuer, an ISD investment firm or a UCITS management company or an authorised person (other than a small company) under the Financial Services and Markets Act 2000.

Where an LLP qualifies as small, it is permitted to prepare its accounts using CA 85, Sch 8 (as amended) which reduces the amount of disclosure required within the accounts. It may also file abbreviated accounts with the Registrar of Companies.

Small LLPs are also able to apply the FRSSE should the members consider this to be appropriate. To the extent that there is a conflict between requirements in the FRSSE and those in the SORP, the FRSSE should have precedence.

Medium-sized LLPs may file abbreviated accounts, although the only difference between these and full financial statements relates to the profit and loss account, which can start with gross profit rather than disclose turnover and cost of sales separately.

Currently a parent LLP need not prepare group accounts for a financial period if it qualifies as a small or medium-sized group and is not an ineligible group as defined above. However, CA 06 will remove the exemption from preparing group accounts conferred on medium-sized groups.

The qualification criteria for being a small or medium-sized group are similar to those for individual companies in that the criteria have to be met:

- in the first financial period, in respect of that period;
- in subsequent periods in both that period and the preceding period; or
- the group needs to have met the qualifying criteria in the preceding period.

The qualifying conditions are as follows:

	Small group
Turnover	Not more than £5.6 million net (or £6.72 million gross)
Balance sheet total	Not more than £2.8 million net (or £3.36 million gross)
Number of employees	Not more than 50
	Medium-sized group
Turnover	Not more than £11.2 million net (or £13.44 million gross)
Balance sheet total	Not more than £5.6 million (or £6.72 million gross)
Number of employees	Not more than 250

10 INTERNATIONAL FINANCIAL REPORTING STANDARDS

2.10 One significant amendment to CA 85 applied to LLPs is the change that permits the use of International Financial Reporting Standards for periods beginning on or after 1 January 2005. The SORP does not deal with the application of IFRS to LLPs and, to date, few LLPs have chosen to prepare their accounts in accordance with IFRS. Where an LLP does choose to use IFRS it must apply all of the standards and the decision will be irrevocable in all but very limited circumstances.

Chapter 3

The LLP and auditor relationship

1 GENERAL REQUIREMENT TO APPOINT AUDITORS

3.1 Unless entitled to the exemptions set out below, all LLPs are required to appoint auditors and have their accounts audited. For the first accounting period, auditors must be appointed before the end of that accounting period. Thereafter, appointment or reappointment for the subsequent year's audit must be made no later than two months after the date of approval of the accounts.

2 EXEMPTION FROM AUDIT

3.2 Exemption from audit is available for LLPs with turnover of £5.6 million or less and a balance sheet total (total assets before taking account of liabilities) that does not exceed £2.8 million. The exemption, however, is not available where the LLP:

- has permission under Part 4 of the Financial Services and Markets Act 2000 to carry on a regulated activity except where the activity is restricted to:
  - arranging regulated mortgage contracts;
  - assisting administration and performance of a contract of insurance;
  - advising on regulated mortgage contacts; or
  - dealing as agent, arranging deals in investments and advising on investments where the activity concerns relevant investments that are not contractually-based investments;
- is carrying on insurance market business; or
- is a parent or a subsidiary unless:
  - throughout the financial period in which it was a subsidiary it was dormant; or

- it is a parent or subsidiary in a small group (see **2.9** for the definition of a small group).

An LLP which is exempt from audit is still required to file accounts with the Registrar of Companies and must also circulate a full set of the accounts to each member.

Entitlement to the exemption is dependent on inclusion on the balance sheet of the statement set out below, which must be inserted immediately above the signature of the designated member(s).

> 'For the financial year ended [ ], the LLP was entitled to exemption from audit under section 249A(1) Companies Act 1985 (as modified for application to LLPs). The members acknowledge their responsibilities for ensuring that the LLP keeps accounting records which comply with section 221 of the Act (as modified) and for preparing accounts which give a true and fair view of the state of affairs of the LLP as at the end of the year and of its profit or loss for the financial year in accordance with the requirements of section 226 (as modified) and which otherwise comply with the requirements of the Companies Act 1985 (as modified), so far as applicable to the LLP.'

3 RESPONSIBILITIES OF MEMBERS AND AUDITORS

3.3 As noted at **2.5** the designated members of the LLP have ultimate responsibility for preparing accounts that give a true and fair view. This responsibility remains the same even in circumstances where the audit firm may have been engaged to assist in the preparation of those accounts.

4 TERMS OF ENGAGEMENT

3.4 The engagement letter issued by the auditor sets out the terms on which the auditor will act and also establishes, in writing, the respective responsibilities of auditors and members. Where the audit firm is to provide other services in addition to the audit (for example, taxation advice), to the extent that these services are also of a recurring nature they may be included in the same letter or may be the subject of a separate letter dependent on the procedures of the audit firm. It is not unusual for the same firm in addition to provide services to individual members. Such services will be covered by separate letters of engagement between the audit firm and the individual member.

As well as detailing the services being provided, the engagement letter will also set out the limitations in the audit process and it is essential that the members understand the scope of the services being provided. The audit firm will ask that a designated member sign a copy of the letter confirming, on behalf of all members, that they understand and agree with the terms.

The recurring nature of the audit appointment means that it may not be necessary to reissue the engagement letter every year. However, as part of their annual planning process, the auditors will reconsider the content of the letter and decide whether it is necessary to reissue it. This may be required where there is a significant change of management, a significant change in the membership of the LLP or a change in any relevant legal or professional requirements.

5 LETTERS OF REPRESENTATION

3.5 Some of the evidence obtained by the auditors will come in the form of oral representations from the management of the LLP. In order to clarify understanding of these representations and to enable the auditors to fully document the evidence upon which their opinion is based the auditors will request written confirmation prior to the audit report being signed. The written representation most usually takes the form of a representation letter to the auditors signed on behalf of the LLP by a designated member. However, on occasions it may be a letter from the auditors outlining their understanding of the representations received, which is then acknowledged and confirmed in writing by the members.

Auditing standards require the auditors to obtain specific written confirmation from the members of the LLP as regards the following:

- That the members acknowledge their responsibility for the design and implementation of controls to prevent and detect fraud and that they have disclosed to the auditors their knowledge of fraud or suspected fraud.
- That the members have disclosed to the auditors any events that involve possible non-compliance with the laws or regulations providing the legal framework within which the LLP conducts its business and which are central to the LLP's ability to conduct its business.
- That information provided regarding the related party and control disclosures in the financial statements is complete. (See Chapter 11 for a further discussion of related parties.)
- An explanation of the reasons for not adjusting any misstatements brought to the attention of the members by the auditors.

These confirmations would usually be included in the letter of representation.

6 THE AUDIT REPORT

3.6 In addition to reporting on whether the accounts of the LLP give a true and fair view, there are certain other matters which legislation requires auditors to report on by exception. These are as follows:

- Whether proper accounting records have been maintained.
- Whether the balance sheet and profit and loss account are in agreement with the accounting records and returns.
- Whether the auditors have obtained all of the information and explanations which they consider to be necessary to enable them to perform their audit.
- Whether information contained in any other information accompanying the financial statements including the members' report is consistent with the accounts.

Auditors are also required to report on the circumstances when financial statements do not comply with applicable accounting standards and the SORP, unless the departure is considered necessary in order for the accounts to give a true and fair view and the accounts contain adequate disclosure of the reasons for the departure.

7 COMMUNICATION BETWEEN THE AUDITOR AND THE LLP

3.7 Auditing standards require auditors to communicate with the members of the LLP on a range of matters including:

- any relationships between the LLP and the audit firm that may affect, or be perceived to affect, the firm's independence;
- the nature and scope of the audit work to be performed;
- the findings from the audit including:
  - the auditor's views about the qualitative aspects of the LLP's accounting practices;
  - the form of representation letter the auditor is requesting from management (see **3.5**);
  - the extent of uncorrected misstatements;
  - any expected modifications to the audit report; and
  - material weaknesses in internal controls identified during the audit.

The communication of material weaknesses is usually in the form of a letter of recommendation to the LLP. The LLP will be requested to include the extent of any action they intend to take as a consequence of the letter of recommendation.

In the UK auditors are always required to communicate the significant findings of the audit. Where there are no significant matters the auditor is required to say so.

The communication from the auditor will also explain that it is restricted to those matters that come to the attention of the audit firm during the course of their work and that the audit is not designed to identify all matters that may be of relevance to the members of the LLP.

8 REGULATORY REPORTS REQUIRED FROM AUDITORS

3.8 In some sectors, for example financial services, additional reports covering an LLP's compliance with regulations are required to be given by the auditors to the regulators. The format of these reports is usually specified by the relevant legislation and, to the extent that it is of a recurring nature, will be covered in the letter of engagement.

In certain regulated businesses, legislation places a duty on auditors to report certain rule breaches, sometimes without the prior knowledge of the entity concerned.

9 REPORTING TO THIRD PARTIES

3.9 From time to time third parties may request reports on certain aspects of the financial information of an LLP. The request may come from a trade body (for example, ABTA), a government department (for example, in relation to a grant application) and a whole range of other possible parties. Provision of such reports goes beyond the statutory duties of an auditor and will always require additional terms of engagement to be agreed.

Dependent on the precise nature of the report the audit firm may require the third party to be included in the engagement letter before it will report to them. Alternatively the audit firm may carry out the assignment directly for the LLP and only allow the third party access to the report after receiving confirmation that the auditors owe no duty of care to that third party.

10 CHANGES IN AUDIT APPOINTMENT

3.10 The procedures surrounding the changes in audit appointment mirror those contained in CA 85 with respect to company audit appointments.

A resigning auditor is required to deposit a written notice of resignation at the registered office of the LLP. The notice of resignation must also be accompanied by a statement setting out any circumstances surrounding the resignation which the auditor considers should be brought to the attention of the members or creditors of the LLP or, where there are no such circumstances, a statement to that effect. The LLP must send a copy of the statement of resignation to the Registrar of Companies no later than 14 days following receipt.

Where the notice of resignation was accompanied by a statement of circumstances, the auditor may lodge, together with his notice of resignation, a requisition calling on the designated members to convene a meeting of the LLP to consider his explanation of the circumstances surrounding the resignation.

The designated members may remove an auditor and appoint a replacement by giving at least seven days' notice to the incumbent auditor. The auditor is entitled to make representations in writing to the LLP and may ask for those representations to be circulated to members. Notice is required to be given to the Registrar of Companies on the prescribed form which can be obtained from Companies House.

Chapter 4

The audit process and auditing standards

1 WHAT IS AN AUDIT?

4.1 The general requirement that the accounts of an LLP are subject to audit has been discussed in Chapter 3. To many, particularly those transferring from partnership to LLP status, whilst they may be aware of the general concepts of audit, the detail may be less familiar. This chapter explains in simple terms what an audit is and the processes and procedures typically performed by auditors.

In general terms, an audit involves the collection and evaluation of evidence on the amounts included within the profit and loss account, balance sheet and notes to the accounts by a suitably qualified, independent person or team of people. Whilst the extent of evidence obtained will vary from audit to audit the intention is that it should be sufficient to enable the auditor to report an opinion as to whether the amounts shown in the accounts give a true and fair view and have been arrived at using generally accepted accounting principles contained within accounting standards and legislation.

2 AUDITING STANDARDS

4.2 The auditors of LLPs are required to carry out their work in accordance with International Standards on Auditing (UK and Ireland) ('auditing standards') which are issued by the Auditing Practices Board. Whilst auditing standards do not dictate the exact nature of the work an auditor should carry out, they do set out both principles and essential procedures which must be applied when carrying out audit work. Individual firms are then able to develop their own methodologies which comply with those auditing standards.

3 THE AUDIT PROCESS

4.3 Whilst the methodologies of individual audit firms vary, all audits can be analysed broadly into the following stages:

- planning;
- fieldwork;
- review; and
- completion and reporting.

4 PLANNING

4.4 Audit firms invest a considerable amount of time on each assignment in ensuring that the work is planned to take full account of the circumstances of the individual client. Planning is essential to developing an approach which is not only effective in minimising the risk that material errors will go undetected by the audit fieldwork, but also makes the most efficient use of audit staff and client time. Auditing standards contain considerable guidance and requirements with respect to the way in which an audit should be planned.

The first stage in the planning process is for the auditors to establish the terms on which they are going to act by issuing an engagement letter (see Chapter 3) or to assess whether the provisions of a letter issued in a previous year are still appropriate. Revisions to the letter will be issued where this is considered to be necessary.

At an early stage the auditors will want to find out about the LLP's business, changes therein and its financial performance during the period together with any significant transactions or other events which may need to be focused on during the audit. In the first year of the auditors' appointment, the amount of information required will be substantially more than in following years as the auditors seek to build up their 'understanding of the business'. This understanding will not just encompass the LLP's business but will also take into account:

- The appropriateness of the selection and application of accounting policies.
- The objectives and strategies of the LLP.
- How the LLP measures and reviews its financial performance.
- The internal controls operated by the LLP including:

  - its overall control environment;
  - its risk assessment process;
  - the information systems and business processes relevant to financial reporting; and
  - controls operated by the LLP and how they are monitored.
- The regulatory framework within which the LLP operates.

The methods adopted to obtain this information will vary but could include meetings, telephone conversations or use of a questionnaire.

Auditing standards specifically require auditors to consider certain matters when they are planning the audit. These include:

- The risk that fraud could give rise to a material error in the accounts. It is the responsibility of the members of the LLP to take reasonable steps to prevent and detect fraud and this responsibility is specifically referred to in the statement of members' responsibilities accompanying the accounts. Therefore, whilst the detection of fraud is outside the role of the auditors, in order to assess fully the risk of a material error in the accounts, they are required to identify and assess the risk of material misstatement due to fraud and evaluate the controls the LLP has in place to mitigate the risk. The auditor is required to discuss the risk of fraud with management and also to obtain information with respect to actual or suspected fraud. To the extent that a risk of misstatement is identified specific audit tests are designed to mitigate that risk.
- Ascertaining whether there are any laws and regulations which provide the legal framework within which the LLP conducts its business and which are central to its ability to conduct that business. Where such laws and regulations are identified evidence of compliance with any such laws or regulations will be sought during the audit. Auditors are not however required to consider all laws and regulations which might be applicable to the LLP.
- Ascertaining the nature of related parties (see Chapter 11) and designing procedures to minimise the risk that the accounts will fail to disclose the existence of a material related party transaction.

Based on the information obtained, the auditors will then develop both an overall plan as to how the audit work should be scoped and detailed work programmes for each area of the accounts. These programmes will then be used by the staff carrying out the fieldwork to guide them through the performance of that work. The audit plan and programmes may be updated during the performance of the work where circumstances are not as envisaged at the time the plan was prepared.

5 MATERIALITY

4.5 In issuing their report on a set of accounts the auditors are not stating that they are correct, but that they contain no 'material' error. Materiality is an expression of the relative significance or importance of a particular matter. Materiality is defined in the following terms:

> 'Information is material if its omission or misstatement could influence the economic decisions of users taken on the basis of the financial statements. Materiality depends on the size of the item or error judged in the particular circumstances of its omission or misstatement. Thus, materiality provides a threshold or cut-off point rather than being a primarily qualitative characteristic which information must have if it is to be useful.'

Materiality is not only considered in the context of the accounts as a whole, but may also be applied in the context of any individual primary statement (profit and loss account and balance sheet) or of individual items included therein. There is no specific mathematical definition of materiality due to the fact that it has both qualitative and quantitative aspects.

At the beginning of the audit, an indicative level of materiality will be calculated, which is usually based on a percentage of turnover, profit or net assets. This serves as a guideline to the auditors to enable them to assess the areas where there is the potential for the greatest risk of material error. Items in the financial statements falling below the calculated materiality figure may be subject to either fewer audit procedures than other areas or, in some cases, no procedures at all.

6 ASSESSMENT OF ACCOUNTING SYSTEMS AND INTERNAL CONTROLS

4.6 The LLP's own systems of internal control and recording of accounting information will influence the audit approach. In some circumstances the auditors may determine that the internal controls that the LLP has in place in a particular area are sufficiently robust to reduce significantly the risk of a material error arising. In these circumstances the auditors may rely on these controls (having first tested them) to reduce the level of their own work. This is known as a compliance approach.

Irrespective of whether the auditors intend to rely on the LLP's own systems and controls, auditing standards require that they obtain an 'understanding' of the information system including the related business processes relevant to financial reporting and of control activities. This usually results in the auditors documenting the key transaction flows of the LLP together with the internal controls operating over those transaction flows. The level of documentation will vary from simple narrative notes through to complex flowcharts, depending on the business of the LLP and, to some extent, the audit methodology of the firm. Some testing will also be carried out to ascertain that the systems operate as documented.

7 OBTAINING AUDIT EVIDENCE

4.7 As part of the planning process, the auditors will have determined the sources from which they will obtain their evidence. The evidence can come from one of three sources: (1) the LLP itself (for example, work in progress calculations), (2) third parties (for example, confirmation of bank balances provided directly to the auditors), or (3) auditor generated (for example, the re-performance of a bank reconciliation). The independent nature of an audit means that third party and auditor generated evidence are considered to be more reliable, but such evidence is also more expensive to obtain. In planning their work, auditors will usually seek to obtain a balance of evidence from all sources, but a level of third party evidence will always be necessary.

There is also more than one way in which the auditor can obtain evidence and the most appropriate method or methods will be adopted for each item in the accounts. The following are the principal categories:

- *Inspection of records or documents*. This tends to be the most commonly used procedure and involves substantiating amounts in the accounting records by reference to documents. Revenue, for example, will be audited in part by agreement to the related contracts and sales invoices together with any proof of delivery of goods or services.
- *Observation and physical inspection.* Whilst in general observation tests are of limited application because they are only valid at a point in time, in some circumstances there is no alternative procedure that can be performed. Probably the most common observation test carried out by auditors is attendance at the stock count of a client where there are material amounts of stock.
- *Inquiry and confirmation.* This covers a wide range of possible tests, from simply seeking clarification from the LLP's staff of something within the accounting records to requesting third party confirmation of items such as bank or sales ledger balances.
- *Recalculation and re-performance*. Re-performance of calculations to check their mathematical accuracy, for example, depreciation calculations or testing ageing of accounts receivable.

- *Analytical procedures.* The analysis of the relationships between amounts included within the accounts, either within the same period, or between comparable amounts from different periods or, in some circumstances, industry statistics.

8 AUDIT WORK PAPERS

4.8 The auditors will record the results of the work performed on work papers which may be manual, electronic or a combination of the two. Auditors are under a professional obligation to safeguard the confidential nature of the work papers and they will not usually allow access to them by any third party, including the members of the LLP.

9 SAMPLING

4.9 Auditors are required to obtain reasonable, but not absolute, assurance as to the amounts included within the accounts. As a result of both this requirement and the need for efficiency, audit evidence is usually obtained on the basis of sample testing. Some audit firms have developed elaborate statistical models to enable them to select their samples whereas other firms take a more judgmental approach. The audit report makes specific reference to the use of sampling.

Irrespective of the precise methods adopted for ascertaining the sample to be tested, there are some general principles to which auditors will always adhere:

- Items are selected in such a way as to give a reasonable expectation that they are representative of the total population. For example, it would be inappropriate to test sales by only looking at transactions in one month. Where there are different types of business within an LLP, samples will need to be selected so that all types of business are covered.
- Selection must be made without any conscious bias—all items should have an equal chance of being selected.
- Where possible the population to be tested should be stratified. A small number of high value items covering a relatively large proportion of the population is usually the most efficient approach.
- Specific key items should be tested—in particular those which are particularly prone to error or misstatement—for example, all debts over a certain age.

10 ERRORS FOUND DURING AUDIT WORK

4.10 Where errors are found by the auditors during the course of their work these will be recorded within the work papers and assessed as to whether or not they are material in the context of the accounts. In making this assessment both the effect of individual errors and the cumulative effect of items which are essentially immaterial will be considered. The auditors will discuss the errors with the members and request that the accounts be amended to deal with those which are, in their opinion, material. The members may choose to process all amendments, but where they decide that this is not necessary, the letter of representation given to the auditors (see **3.5**) will need to explain the reasons for non-adjustment – namely that in the opinion of the members they are not considered to affect the view given by the accounts.

11 REVIEW

4.11 Auditing standards require that all work papers be reviewed by a member of the team who is more experienced than the preparer. Reviewing the audit file not only ensures that the work carried out is sufficient to enable an audit opinion to be given, but also ensures that those not involved in the day-to-day work (typically the manager and partner) are aware of all issues affecting the LLP. The partner who will sign the audit opinion is not required to review all working papers but at a minimum the review must cover critical areas of judgement, significant risks and other areas they consider to be important.

12 COMPLETION OF THE AUDIT

4.12 In addition to ensuring that all the audit work has been completed satisfactorily, there are a number of other procedures that the auditors are required to carry out prior to issuing their report. These will include the following:

- Discussing with the members the extent to which there have been any events subsequent to the completion of their fieldwork and through to the date of their report which provide additional evidence as to any of the amounts included within the accounts.
- Ascertaining whether there have been any changes in circumstances which might affect the members' assessment of whether the LLP is a going concern. The concept of going concern is discussed in more detail in Chapter 12.
- Obtaining the letter of representation from the members.

13 THE AUDIT OPINION

4.13 Chapter 3 sets out the general requirement that an audit report should contain the auditors' opinion as to whether or not the accounts give a true and fair view. Where the auditors have not been able to obtain all of the information they require ('limitation of scope') or they disagree with the treatment or disclosure of an item in the accounts a qualified audit report is issued. The qualification can take a number of forms:

- *Adverse opinion.* Where the auditors consider that the matter with which they disagree is so material or all pervasive that the accounts are misleading. In these circumstances the audit opinion will state that the accounts do not give a true and fair view.
- *Disclaimer.* When the possible effect of a limitation in scope is so material or pervasive that the auditors have not been able to obtain sufficient evidence to enable them to form an opinion on the accounts.
- *'Except for'.* Where the auditors have been unable to obtain sufficient evidence with respect to one or more items, but where they are satisfied with the evidence available in all other areas. This form of opinion is also used where the auditors disagree with the accounting treatment or disclosure in relation to an item in the accounts.

In certain circumstances there may be uncertainties surrounding an amount in the accounts, where the effect of the possible range of outcomes could be material. In these circumstances the auditors will make reference to the existence of *'significant uncertainty'* in their report by way of an emphasis of matter paragraph, but this does not, however, constitute a qualification of the audit report.

Chapter 5

Remuneration of members and employees, division of profit and members' balances

1 MEMBERS' INTERESTS AS FINANCIAL INSTRUMENTS

5.1 Probably the single biggest change to affect LLPs between the original SORP and the revised version came as a consequence of FRS 25 'Financial instruments: presentation and disclosure' and UITF 39 'Members' shares in co-operative entities and similar instruments'. The definition of financial instruments is so widely drawn that the various rights members have to participate in an LLP whether by way of capital or sharing of profits fall within the requirements of these standards.

FRS 25 has applied for all accounting periods that began on or after 1 December 2005 and, amongst other things, requires that financial instruments be classified between liabilities and equity (the term used for residual interests) by reference to substance rather than legal form. The definition of equity is very tightly drawn and unless an entity has an unconditional right to withhold payment to an instrument holder unpaid amounts are classed as a liability and related returns as an expense.

The implications for LLPs are therefore wide ranging and each LLP needs to examine its members' agreement carefully to determine whether balances due to members are 'equity' or a liability and whether arrangements to share profits might constitute an expense of the LLP.

2 THE NATURE OF MEMBERS' REMUNERATION

5.2 The way in which members are remunerated will vary between LLPs but will reflect the fact that the members are in the position of both owning the LLP and, usually, working within it. In a company environment the distinction between the rewards a director receives by virtue of ownership (dividends) and those received for services provided (emoluments) are more readily distinguished, but within an LLP the distinction between the two is frequently blurred. The accounting treatment and presentation of amounts payable to members is not determined by whether the payments are rewards for working in the LLP or ownership thereof, but by whether or not the LLP has discretion over payment of the amounts.

Members may obtain reward for their involvement with the LLP through one or a combination of the following:

- *Salaried remuneration.* Due to the HMRC interpretation that members of an LLP should, by default, be treated as self-employed, it is relatively unusual for members to receive an entitlement to profit through an employment contract.
- *Fixed share.* Members may be 'guaranteed' a certain amount of remuneration each year either within the membership agreement or through individual arrangements between the LLP and the member. This amount will be paid to them irrespective of the level of profits made by the LLP.
- *Share in residual profit.* Members are awarded a share of the profit made by the LLP, after the payment of any salaried remuneration and fixed shares. The basis of allocation will vary but will typically be based on a formula linked to the capital introduced by the member. Other factors such as seniority may also be included within the calculation. Often, members will be entitled to a fixed amount, as well as a share in residual profit.
- *Drawings.* While salaried remuneration, fixed shares and residual shares refer to the member's entitlement to profit, drawings refer to the cash payments received in respect of that entitlement. Depending on the terms of the members' agreement, drawings may be paid in respect of profit to which the member is already entitled, or may be paid in advance of the division of profit to the member.

3 ACCOUNTING FOR MEMBERS' REMUNERATION

5.3 The SORP's treatment of members' remuneration and profit share, and the related balance sheet items, reflects the presentation requirements of FRS 25.

The way in which members' remuneration is accounted for depends on whether it falls to be treated as an expense of the LLP in the period or whether it relates to current period profit that, at the year end, is still available for discretionary division among the members.

The amended LLPR 2001 require that the profit and loss account discloses a total for 'Profit or loss for the financial year before members' remuneration and profit share'. Members' remuneration charged as an expense should be shown immediately after this, with the remainder being profit or loss available for discretionary division among members.

Paragraph 44 of the SORP requires the following disclosure to be made on the face of the profit and loss account.

Profit or loss for the financial year before members' remuneration and profit shares	X
Members' remuneration charged as an expense	(X)
Profit or loss for the financial year available for discretionary division among members	X

In determining the amount which is charged as an expense, both the amounts payable to the member and any associated employment costs should be included.

4 IDENTIFYING REMUNERATION CHARGED AS AN EXPENSE

5.4 In determining whether amounts paid to members during an accounting period from that period's profit should be treated as an expense, the SORP considers whether the LLP has the unconditional right to repayment of these amounts from the members at the balance sheet date. If it does not, the amounts are treated as an expense.

For profit that has not yet been paid to members at the year end, the SORP considers whether the LLP has the unconditional right to withhold those amounts from members at the balance sheet date. If it does not, the amounts are again treated as an expense.

Unpaid profits for the year that the LLP has the unconditional right to withhold (and drawn profits for the year that the LLP has the unconditional right to reclaim) at the balance sheet date are treated as available for discretionary division.

In practical terms, remuneration charged as an expense comprises the following:

- *Drawings made from current year profit, of which the LLP does not have the unconditional right to demand repayment at the year end.* This will include salaried remuneration and fixed profit shares. Where the members' agreement stipulates that payments on account of residual profit cannot be reclaimed, except to the extent amounts paid exceed the member's profit division for the year, payments of residual profit made in the year are also treated as an expense.

- *Undrawn profit, which the LLP does not have the unconditional right to withhold from the members at the year end.* This will include, for example, profit-related bonuses to which members are entitled, either through a contract with the LLP or the members' agreement. All undrawn profit will be treated as an expense if, for example, the members' agreement requires that profit for each year must be fully distributed.

Profit available for discretionary division among members comprises the following:

- *Drawings made from current year profit, of which the LLP has the unconditional right to demand repayment at the year end.* This will occur where payments on account of residual profit are made, and the members' agreement stipulates that no residual profit is divided among the members until some process of post year end approval has taken place.
- *Undrawn profit, which the LLP has the unconditional right to withhold from the members at the year end.* This will relate to undrawn residual profit, the division of which is subject to post year end approval.

The following table, reproduced from paragraph 47 of the SORP, summarises the treatment of members' remuneration:

Nature of element of member's remuneration	**Treat as**
Remuneration that is paid under an employment contract	Expense, described as 'Members' remuneration charged as an expense', and deducted after arriving at 'Profit for the financial year before members' remuneration and profit shares'
Other payments, arising from components of members' participation rights in the profits for the year that give rise to liabilities in accordance with FRS 25 and UITF 39, such as mandatory interest payments	
Automatic division of profits	

Nature of element of member's remuneration	Treat as
Any share of profits arising from a division of profits that is discretionary on the part of the LLP (ie where the decision to divide the profits is taken after the profits have been made)	Allocation of profits

When profit available for discretionary division among members is subsequently divided, there is no impact on the profit and loss account, and the movement is reflected in the reconciliation of movements in members' interests, of which an example is provided at **5.10**. The balance sheet treatment of amounts paid and payable to members and of undivided profit is explained at **5.6**.

For a large proportion of LLPs the remuneration of members will comprise both an expense element and an allocation of profits, which will need to be separately recorded and accounted for.

In addition to impacting its presentation in the profit and loss account and balance sheet, the extent to which members receive remuneration that falls to be treated as an expense affects the valuation of work in progress. Remuneration charged as an expense will need to be included within the calculation of work in progress whereas discretionary profit allocation will be excluded. Accounting for work in progress is considered in more detail in Chapter 8.

The SORP requires disclosure of the way in which each type of remuneration has been determined and accounted for and it may be most appropriate to include this within the accounting policy note.

5 THE COMPOSITION OF MEMBERS' INTERESTS

5.5 Within the balance sheet, amounts relating to the interaction of the LLP with its members can give rise to three types of balance:

- *Amounts due from members.* Amounts which are debts owed by the members to the LLP, for example, drawings paid in excess of profit entitlement.
- *Loans and other debts due to members.* Amounts which are liabilities owed by the LLP to the members, for example, undrawn profit allocations and capital introduced by the members where they are entitled to

repayment on retirement. The latter is a liability because the LLP cannot avoid payment.

- *Equity*. Includes only those amounts that the LLP has the unconditional right to withhold from the members, for example, undistributed profits that the LLP has the right to retain, capital introduced by members whose repayment is subject to approval, and unallocated revaluation reserves.

6 PRESENTATION OF MEMBERS' INTERESTS WITHIN THE ACCOUNTS

5.6 The presentation of members' balances required by the SORP reflects the presentation elements of FRS 25, which deal with the classification of financial instruments between debt and equity.

Members' balances are treated as equity only if the LLP has the unconditional right to withhold them from the member (or, in the case of amounts that have been paid to members, if the LLP has the unconditional right to reclaim them). Otherwise they are treated as a liability due to the member. An example is provided at **5.7**.

Under the SORP, all members' balances in the LLP, whether equity or a liability, are shown within 'net assets attributable to members', on the 'bottom half' of the balance sheet. This treatment differs from a company balance sheet, where only equity balances are included in the bottom half of the balance sheet, and all liabilities are shown in the top half as a deduction from net assets. As a consequence any LLP which has zero equity (because, for example, all capital must be returned and all profits are automatically divided) does not present a balance sheet that totals zero but one that shows the net assets attributable to members. The presentation of members' interests is further illustrated in the example accounts in Appendix 1.

The treatment of members' balances in an LLP may also differ from the treatment of partners' balances adopted by general partnerships. Many partnerships show all credit balances with partners in the bottom half of the balance sheet, regardless of whether they are debt or equity, which results in similar presentation to that recommended for LLPs. However, in some general partnerships partners' tax balances are shown in the top half of the balance sheet and this differs from the treatment under the SORP where they form part of 'net assets attributable to members'.

A further area of difference that may arise between a general partnership and an LLP is where an individual partner owes money to the partnership. In a general partnership, these balances are often accounted for as negative amounts in the bottom half of the balance sheet. However, in an LLP 'net assets attributable to members' can only include members' balances in the LLP, and negative amounts owed by the member to the LLP cannot be offset, unless the member has the legal right to offset the balance against other balances. Amounts owed by the member to the LLP are separately disclosed within debtors in the top half of the balance sheet.

The SORP also requires that total members' interests be presented in the accounts by showing the sum of amounts due from members, amounts due to members and members' other interests as a memorandum item on the balance sheet. This is illustrated in the example at **5.7**.

The presentation of amounts within 'net assets attributable to members' in an LLP also differs from the presentation of partners' balances that is normally adopted in a general partnership. In a general partnership, balances would normally be categorised by their purpose (capital, current, taxation, etc). In an LLP, they are first categorised by whether they are equity or debt, and then subcategorised between capital and other amounts. For example, in an LLP there is no difference in disclosure between current account balances and taxation balances that are payable to or on behalf of members; both are included within 'loans and other debts due to members – other amounts'.

7 CLASSIFICATION OF PROFIT IN THE BALANCE SHEET

5.7 The basis on which profits are allocated to individual members will be governed by the members' agreement. The issue that arises is when the profits made by the LLP become a liability due to the members and when they should be classified as equity.

The balance sheet treatment follows the treatment in the profit and loss account, which is explained at **5.4**.

Profit which forms part of 'profit available for discretionary distribution among members' in the profit and loss account should be treated as equity. To the extent that drawings have been made against profit that is included within equity (which is the case where the LLP has the unconditional right to reclaim drawings), these drawings are shown as 'other debts due from members' within debtors.

Members' remuneration charged as an expense represents profit that the LLP does not have the unconditional right to withhold from the members, and, to the extent it has not been drawn, is presented as a liability due to members in the balance sheet. Where profit that was available for discretionary distribution at the end of the previous year has been divided among the members in the current year, but has not yet been paid, this is also presented as a liability.

The policy for division of profit can significantly impact the shape of an LLP's balance sheet, as demonstrated in the example below.

Example

The firm has made 350 units of profit for the year, of which 250 have been drawn in the year and 100 remain undrawn.

- In firm A, all profit is automatically divided (ie the firm does not have the unconditional right to withhold any profit made from the members), and the undrawn profit of 100 units is presented within loans and other debts due to members.
- In firm B, drawn profit is divided and cannot be reclaimed by the firm, but the division of undrawn profit is subject to post year end approval. The undrawn profit of 100 units is presented within equity.
- In firm C, division of all profit is subject to post year end approval. All 350 units of profit are presented within equity and the 250 units that have been drawn are presented as 'amounts due from members'.

In all three firms, members are entitled to repayment of their capital on retirement, so, in each case, members' capital is presented within 'loans and other debts due to members', rather than 'equity'. Members' capital is discussed in more detail at **5.8**.

	A	**B**	**C**
Cash	200	200	200
Trade debtors	100	100	
Amounts due from members	–	–	250
Trade creditors	(100)	(100)	(100)
Net assets attributable to members	200	200	450

	A	B	C
Loans and other debt due to members			
Members' capital	100	100	100
Other amounts	100	–	–
	200	100	100
Equity			
Members' other interests	–	100	350
	200	200	450
Total members' interests			
Amounts due from members	–	–	(250)
Loans and other debts due to members	200	100	100
Equity	–	100	350
	200	200	200

8 ACCOUNTING RECORDS

5.8 While the published LLP accounts will only show members' interests at an aggregated level, the accounting records maintained with respect to members' interests will need to contain sufficient detail to be able to ascertain the financial relationship between each member and the LLP. They will therefore need to include details of the capital introduced by the member, profits allocated, any salaries paid and drawings made.

9 MEMBERS' CAPITAL

5.9 All members of an LLP will be required to contribute capital, although there is a wide variation in the policies of individual LLPs as to how this is achieved. The contribution of capital will occur both at the stage of initial admission as a member and at subsequent dates.

Capital may be contributed either in cash or through an arrangement whereby a member agrees to 'capitalise' part of their profit allocation for the year. The latter might typically happen on initial admission when it might be agreed that the member could reach their capital requirement over a number of years.

Unlike a limited company, an LLP is able to repay to the members any of its capital or convert it to debt without any legal restrictions on 'capital maintenance', and the terms and conditions attaching to members' capital will be determined by the members' agreement. Whilst this appears to create greater flexibility, in practice it is probable that restrictions will arise as a result of external requirements placed on the LLP to maintain a certain level of capital (for example, by bankers). LLPs repaying capital will also need to be aware of the risk of this being viewed as a preference over creditors in the event of the LLP subsequently running into financial difficulties and becoming insolvent.

In the same way as for profits, the accounting classification of members' capital between equity and debt depends on whether the LLP has the unconditional right to withhold repayment to the members. Where the members' agreement entitles a member to the return of capital on retirement from the LLP, the capital is classified as a debt due to members.

Prior to the SORP, the majority of members' agreements provided for an automatic return of capital on retirement. However, in practice, in a thriving firm, it would be normal for capital repaid to retiring members to be replaced by newly admitted members or increased capital contributions by existing members. Some firms have chosen to formalise this arrangement, by amending their members' agreements to state that capital will be returned to members on retirement, subject to the firm retaining a specified minimum level of capital. This minimum level would fall to be treated as equity under the revised SORP.

The terms attaching to capital have wider implications than purely accounting. Where the LLP has the right to refuse capital payments that reduce total capital below a minimum level, this increases the rights of the LLP relative to the individual members. If, for example, the firm faced difficult times and an outflow of members, the right of the LLP to hold a minimum level of capital would reduce the extent to which a withdrawal of the firm's working capital would compound the effect of the loss of key fee-earners.

10 RECONCILIATION OF MOVEMENT IN MEMBERS' INTERESTS

5.10 The SORP requires the accounts of the LLP to include a comprehensive statement of the components of members' interests and movements during the year. An example is provided below:

	Members' equity interests				Loans and other debts due to members			
	Members' capital classed as	**Revaluation reserve**	**Other reserves**	**Total**	**Members' capital classed as**	**Other amounts**	**Total**	**Total**
Amounts due to members						X		
Amounts due from members						(X)		
Members' interests at [date]	X	X	X	X	X	X	X	X
Members' remuneration charged as an expense						X	X	X
Profit/(loss) for the financial year available for discretionary			X	X				X
Members' interests after profit/(loss) for the year	X	X	X	X	X	X	X	X
Other divisions of profits/ (losses)			(X)	(X)		X	X	
Surplus arising on revaluation of fixed assets		X		X				X
Introduced by members					X		X	X
Repayments of capital					(X)		(X)	(X)
Repayment of debt						(X)	(X)	(X)
Drawings						(X)	(X)	(X)
Other movements	X	X	X	X	X	X	X	X
Amounts due to members							X	
Amounts due from members							(X)	
Members' interests [date]	X	X	X	X	X	X	X	X

11 BORROWINGS OF MEMBERS

5.11 Within partnerships it is common practice for the partners to borrow in order to fund their interests in that partnership. These arrangements frequently involve the partnership entering into a guarantee, indemnity or similar arrangement with the provider of the funding. Similar arrangements arise in LLPs.

The fact that the members' interests have been funded by way of borrowings is not of itself something which requires disclosure in the accounts. Instead it is necessary to look at the extent of the LLP's obligation to the provider of finance and how this should be treated.

It would be unusual to include a provision in the accounts for the amount of any such loan. FRS 12 would only require a provision to be recognised when the LLP had a legal or constructive obligation to repay the loan and the requirement for repayment was probable at the year end. Circumstances where this might arise include the death or early retirement through ill-health of a member. In determining the amount of any provision, the LLP should take into account the extent to which it is legally entitled to offset the liability against the capital interests and other debts due to the member. In addition, in certain circumstances, such as the death of a member, the repayment may be covered by insurance.

Where it is unlikely that the guarantee or indemnity will be called, its existence should be disclosed as a contingent liability in the notes to the accounts.

12 MEMBERS' REMUNERATION DISCLOSURES

5.12 In addition to the requirement to disclose members' remuneration charged as an expense separately on the face of the profit and loss account, LLPR 2001 and the SORP require a number of additional disclosures to be made in the notes to the accounts.

The average number of members during the year should be disclosed in a note to the accounts. Whilst not required by either LLPR 2001 or the SORP, the members may wish to include details of average members' remuneration. Where this option is taken, the SORP states that it should be calculated by reference to the disclosed average number of members and the amount of 'profit before members' remuneration and profit shares' shown in the profit and loss account.

Where there are factors which distort the amount of profit attributable to members in the year (for example adjustments to retirement benefits) the members are allowed to disclose an adjusted average members' remuneration provided that a reconciliation between the basic and adjusted calculations is provided.

Where the profit of the LLP before members' remuneration and profit shares is greater than £200,000, the notes to the accounts are required to disclose the remuneration of the member with the highest entitlement to profit. As well as entitlements from the LLP, this will also include any amounts paid to the member by a subsidiary undertaking or other third party. The SORP does not specify how the amount should be calculated, as the most appropriate method may vary depending on differences in remuneration structures between LLPs. However, the SORP does require that the method of calculation should be disclosed, and that a consistent policy should be applied year on year. The 'highest paid' member does not have to be named.

Where part of the 'highest paid' member's remuneration is paid by a subsidiary which is a limited company, the amount to be included is calculated by reference to the CA 85 definition of emoluments and will, therefore, include the monetary value of any benefits in kind. In addition, any contributions paid by the subsidiary to a money purchase pension scheme on behalf of the highest paid member will need to be disclosed in the accounts of the LLP.

Where it is considered that it will assist an understanding of the financial performance of the LLP, the SORP recommends that members' remuneration charged as an expense should be further analysed within the notes to the financial statements, for example, between that which is paid under a contract of employment and that which relates to amounts arising from participation rights that give rise to a liability.

13 DISCLOSURE OF MEMBERS' BALANCES

5.13 The extent to which members' balances should be disclosed as equity or as 'loans and other debts due to members' is discussed above.

LLPR 2001 require separate disclosure of the aggregate amount of money advanced by the members by way of loan, the aggregate amount of money owed to members in respect of profits and any other amounts. To the extent that this information is not ascertainable from the reconciliation of movements in members' interests, additional disclosure should be made. The total amount due after more than one year should also separately be disclosed.

In addition, the SORP requires that the notes to the accounts disclose where amounts due to members would rank on a winding up in relation to other unsecured creditors. In the absence of any agreement to the contrary, amounts due to members will rank equally with other creditors. This position may, however, make it difficult for the LLP to obtain credit from third parties, and the LLP may choose to subordinate all or part of the debt due to the members to other creditors in the event of a winding up.

The members' report should include details of the policies adopted by the LLP with respect to capital maintenance. This includes a discussion of the policies adopted in dealing with members' drawings and how these are managed when they come into conflict with the cash requirements of the LLP.

The policy under which members make contributions of equity or debt to the LLP and the terms of their repayment should be disclosed. The members' report must also include details of equity which has been converted to debt (and vice versa) both within the year and for the period from the year end up until the date the accounts are approved.

14 EMPLOYEE COSTS

5.14 For a number of LLPs, particularly those arising on transfer from an existing partnership in the services sector, staff costs are likely to constitute one of the largest expenses in the profit and loss account.

The costs of employment of staff should be included within the appropriate heading in the profit and loss account. Staff costs include not only the amounts paid by way of salaries or wages but also employers' National Insurance, pension contributions and bonuses.

15 DISCLOSURES IN RESPECT OF EMPLOYEES

5.15 A note to the accounts should include the amounts of salaries and wages paid to employees, the amount of social security costs (National Insurance in the case of UK employees) and pension contributions. Where an LLP pays remuneration to its members under an employment contract, these amounts should also be included.

The average number of staff employed (including members who have an employment contract) is also required to be disclosed. This figure, which is also used as the basis of the number of employees in determining whether an LLP is small or medium-sized (see Chapter 2), is calculated by taking the number of employees each month and dividing by 12. It should be noted that the figure for average number of employees is determined by reference to the total number in employment and not by how many hours they work – the use of 'full-time equivalents' is not permitted.

Chapter 6

Retirement benefits

1 INTRODUCTION

6.1 The accounting treatment of retirement benefits within LLPs is probably one of the most complex areas. The accounting requirements with respect to retiring members, in particular, have been the subject of much debate and changed substantially in the 2006 version of the SORP compared to the original version.

2 RETIREMENT BENEFITS OF EMPLOYEES

6.2 Where retirement benefits are provided to employees under an occupational pension scheme this will most probably be through one of two types of scheme:

- *Defined contribution scheme (often called a money purchase scheme).* In this type of scheme the employee and/or the employer pays regular contributions fixed as an amount or percentage of pay and has no obligation to pay further contributions if the scheme has insufficient assets to pay all employee benefits relating to employee service in the current and prior periods. Individual benefits are determined by reference to the contributions paid into the scheme in respect of the employee.
- *Defined benefit scheme (also called a final salary scheme).* This is a scheme where normally the rules specify the benefits to be paid (usually based on the employee's average or final pay) and the scheme is financed accordingly.

Accounting for the provision of benefits under defined contribution schemes is reasonably straightforward—the employer's cost recorded in the profit and loss account comprises the contributions payable.

Where an employing LLP does not have an occupational pension scheme, but makes contributions to the personal pension plans of individuals, these contributions are also accounted for as they are paid.

6.2 *Retirement benefits*

For a defined benefit scheme, the situation is far more complex, because the benefits to be paid are dependent on future events, such as the average or final pay of the employee and the remaining lifetime of both the active and pensioner members of the scheme.

For periods beginning on or after 1 January 2005, LLPs are required to account for any defined, benefit pension schemes in accordance with FRS 17 'Retirement benefits'.

In summary, FRS 17 requires the following:

- Scheme assets to be valued at fair value at the LLP's balance sheet date.
- The scheme liabilities to be valued using the projected unit method discounted using a high quality corporate bond rate.
- The net pension asset or surplus to be shown on the balance sheet. Whilst a liability will nearly always be included, a surplus is only included to the extent that the employer will benefit either as a result of reduced contributions or refunds from the scheme.
- The profit and loss charge is analysed between:
    - Amounts included within operating costs:
        - current service costs;
        - past service costs;
        - any previously unrecognised surplus deducted from past service costs;
        - gains or losses on settlements and curtailments; and
        - any previously unrecognised surplus deducted from the settlement or curtailment of losses.
    - Amounts included within financing costs and shown adjacent to interest:
        - interest costs (the unwinding of the discount on the scheme liabilities); and
        - expected return on assets.

Actuarial gains and losses are accounted for through the STRGL.

There is also a significant level of disclosure required in the notes to the accounts including information about the underlying actuarial assumptions.

The surplus or, more frequently, deficit is required to be shown separately on the face of the balance sheet.

First time adoption of FRS 17 requires a prior year adjustment to comparatives, and this has caused a number of LLPs a very specific problem not found in similar situations for companies. Where there is a deficit recognised on the 'top' half of the balance sheet, an equivalent amount needs to be recorded within the reserves sides of the balance sheet. In the corporate model this is straightforward and is deducted from the profit and loss reserve. However, LLPs do not accumulate a profit and loss reserve in the same way and all previous profits may well have been distributed. Many LLPs have solved the problem by creating an additional category within members' interests.

The requirements of FRS 17 are onerous and forward planning is essential on the part of both those preparing the accounts and those carrying out the audit. Much of the information will probably need to be produced by the actuaries to the pension scheme who will also need reasonable notice of what information is required.

There are a number of factors which need to be considered which include:

- The LLP and its pension scheme may have different year ends. The consequences of this are that it will not be possible to rely on the scheme's accounts to ascertain asset values and the actuarial information may well also need to be prepared to a different date.
- Access may be required by the auditors to the scheme records in order to carry out procedures on movements since the last set of audited accounts. Where the trustees will not permit this or it is considered more efficient, it may be necessary to involve the auditors of the pension scheme.
- The actuarial method required by FRS 17 may differ from that used by the actuaries when determining the funding rate of the scheme and could result in the need for two different valuations.
- There will be additional costs for both preparing the actuarial information and auditing the disclosures.
- Defined benefit type schemes held by any overseas subsidiaries will need to be accounted for in the same way if consolidated accounts are being prepared.

3 RETIREMENT BENEFITS TO CURRENT MEMBERS

6.3 Where members have an employment contract (see Chapter 5) and have retirement benefits which are awarded based on the remuneration received under those contracts, those benefits should be accounted for in the same way as for employees (see above).

6.3 *Retirement benefits*

Other retirement benefits payable to members in the future (often referred to as annuities) will usually be of one of the following:

- *Predetermined.* An amount which is fixed at the time of retirement (annuity). This may, for example, be by reference to the profits earned in the last year of membership. Alternatively, it could be a fixed sum, which may be index-linked or linked to some other measure which is independent of the profits of the LLP.
- *Profit-dependent.* An amount which effectively results in the member continuing to receive a share in the profits of the LLP post retirement. There is a wide range of methods used for providing profit-dependent benefits and these may include arrangements whereby the LLP has to achieve a certain level of profits before any payment is made. In addition, a maximum level of benefit payable may be imposed either by reference to a percentage of profits or monetary amount.

A combination of the two types of benefit is also possible. For example, a retiring member may be entitled to a lump sum payment based on a factor such as past profits and an additional amount in future years based on the profits of the LLP. The period of time for which the benefit will be paid may also vary.

Details of the retirement benefits of members will usually be found in the membership agreement. This will require careful review to ensure that all benefits have been identified and correctly accounted for. The membership agreement may not however contain all details of retirement benefits and a constructive obligation may have arisen as a result of either custom and practice or discussions held with individual members. These will also need to be considered when determining the accounting treatment of members' retirement benefits.

The previous version of the SORP did not require any recognition of the liability to make payments to retired members until the time a member retired. At this point an estimate of the future liability was made and recognised in the balance sheet and was treated as an arrangement amongst members not affecting the profit and loss account. Many commentators noted that this treatment was not in accordance with the way in which retirement benefits are generally accounted for and seemed at odds with general accounting principles.

In the 2006 version of the SORP this apparent anomaly has been addressed with a different, and more consistent, accounting treatment being required.

The SORP requires that the principles of FRS 25 and FRS 12 'Provisions, contingent liabilities and contingent assets' be applied to the accounting for retirement benefits of members.

The nature of the uncertainties associated with retirement benefits, however, means that more arrangements are likely to fall under the provisions of FRS 12 than they will FRS 25. An annuity would meet the definition of a financial liability under FRS 25 if there is a contractual obligation for the LLP to deliver cash or a financial asset to a member. The SORP includes as an example of a retirement benefit that would be accounted for under FRS 25 an annuity where the former member is paid a fixed annual amount for a fixed term beginning on the first anniversary of his retirement, and where, if he dies during the fixed term, an amount representing the present value of the future payments is paid to his estate.

Applying the principles of FRS 12 means that an annuity should be recognised once the member has an actual or constructive right to receive it, and the LLP has no discretion to withhold payment.

It is most usually the case that the rights to receive an annuity arise over time (ie whilst the member continues to be a member of the LLP) and it follows, therefore, that the liability should be accrued over that period, building up a liability through to the time of retirement rather than, as with the previous version of the SORP, recognising it only when the member retires.

In many cases the member may only obtain absolute entitlement to an annuity on reaching a specific milestone, for example achieving a specified number of years service. Even in these circumstances, because the LLP cannot avoid the liability that is accruing in the period through to reaching entitlement, the liability should be built up over the total period of service.

4 CALCULATION OF THE PROVISION

6.4 The liability that is recognised in the accounts should be based on the expectations as at the balance sheet date of:

- the likely date the member will cease to be a member; and
- the amounts likely to be payable to him or her from that date.

The introduction of age-discrimination legislation and its effect on retirement clauses in contracts of employment or membership agreements, however, could mean that it is now more difficult to estimate when someone will cease to be a member.

LLPs with profit-dependent retirement benefit schemes will have to make an assessment of their future profits in order to determine the level of provision. Whilst there will have to be a certain amount of subjectivity attached to these estimates it should be possible for the LLP to determine the range of potential outcomes from which a provision could be calculated.

In determining the value of the liability for members' retirement benefits it will often be appropriate to use the principles of FRS 17 and therefore to seek the advice of an actuary who will be able to provide details of factors to be taken into account, such as life expectancy. Where this is probable, in a similar way to obtaining FRS 17 information for the LLP's accounts, the actuary will need to be contacted well in advance of preparing the accounts and the auditors will also need to be made aware of the need for their involvement.

The liability needs to be recalculated on an annual basis to take account of changes in membership, eligibility for post-retirement payments, financial estimates and actuarial assumptions.

5 PRESENTATION OF MEMBERS' RETIREMENT BENEFITS

6.5 The amounts that are recognised in the profit and loss account with respect to current members should be included within 'Members' remuneration charged as an expense'. The change in liability in respect of former members, however, should not be included within 'Members' remuneration charged as an expense' but within the relevant profit and loss heading – for example 'Administration expenses'.

The liability in the balance sheet with respect to former members should be described as 'Post-retirement payments to former members' and included either within 'Provisions for liabilities' or 'Creditors' dependent upon the circumstances.

The liability with respect to current members should be included within 'Loans and other debts due to members' and be described separately where the amount is material. In the year a member retires, the liability should be transferred and included within balances in respect of former members.

Where former members are awarded amounts with respect to past service after their retirement date, this should be recognised in full in the profit and loss account at the time the award is made.

The LLP should also disclose the accounting policy adopted with respect to retirement benefits.

6 INVESTMENTS HELD TO FUND FUTURE RETIREMENT BENEFITS

6.6 Historically, the liability for retirement benefits within partnerships has been unfunded as it would be met from future profits. Whilst the amounts involved mean that LLPs are unlikely to make investments of a size that will cover the liability in the accounts, they may, for example, make investments to meet requirements to fund retirements in the near future. Any such investments should be included on the balance sheet as investments, but be separately identified in the notes.

7 SPECIFIC ISSUES ON CONVERSION TO AN LLP

6.7 The relationship between the LLP and any predecessor entity will need to be carefully considered. The LLP may assume responsibility for the retirement benefits of a predecessor partnership or other organisation and in these circumstances, where a legal or constructive obligation exists to pay those amounts, it should be recognised as a provision in the accounts of the LLP.

More commonly, on transition, the predecessor entity may transfer those liabilities to a third party (for example, an insurance company). In these circumstances the former partners or directors may only have recourse to the LLP in the event of the failure of that third party. To the extent that there has been no default and none is probable, the existence of the right of recourse should be disclosed as a contingent liability in the accounts.

Chapter 7

Taxation

1 INTRODUCTION

7.1 Whilst this book deals principally with accounting requirements, the taxation of LLPs and its members cannot be entirely ignored. This chapter aims only to give a brief overview of the taxation of LLPs and cover some areas where the taxation treatment may differ from the accounts. It should not be regarded as comprehensive advice and reference should be had to taxation specialists where appropriate.

2 BASIC TAX PRINCIPLES AND COMPLIANCE PROCEDURES

7.2 An LLP is not in itself subject to tax but is, as described by HM Revenue & Customs (HMRC), a 'transparent' entity, which means that the LLP is 'looked through' and its members are subject to tax. Each member will be taxed directly on his share of the LLP's profits, including a share of any investment income earned by the LLP, and on the proceeds received from any capital assets. Members are also liable to Class II and Class IV National Insurance contributions.

Despite the fact that the LLP is not itself liable to tax, it must complete a tax return for each fiscal year. Fiscal years run from 6 April in one year to 5 April in the following year. There are special rules that apply on the commencement of a business, but in general the tax return will include the results for the accounting period ended within the fiscal year. For example if an LLP has a 30 June year end, the 2007/08 return (covering the period 6 April 2007 to 5 April 2008) would include results for the accounting period ended 30 June 2007. Investment income which has been taxed at source, proceeds from the disposal of capital assets and charges on income are however included in the tax return on the basis of the fiscal year in which they arose.

In addition to the general requirement to retain accounting records discussed in Chapter 2, the LLP must also maintain any additional records relating to the tax position for five years and ten months following the end of the tax year in which the accounting period ended.

The tax return must be signed by a designated member to confirm that the information shown thereon is correct and complete. The designated member will be responsible for any penalties arising as a result of non-compliance with HMRC procedures. At the date of publication, the following penalties could be applied by HMRC:

- Late submission of LLP return—£100 *per member.**
- Incorrect LLP return—up to 100 per cent of the tax lost.
- Failure to keep and maintain records—£3,000 *per member.*

* If the failure to submit the return extends beyond six months of the filing deadline a further £100 per member may be levied.

Whilst certain penalties may sometimes be negotiated with HMRC, the penalties for late submission of a return are mandatory and can be substantial depending upon the size of the firm. In view of this, the designated member signing the tax return may wish to ask his fellow members to indemnify him against such penalties.

The tax return must be filed with HMRC by 31 January following the end of the fiscal year. For example the 2007/08 return must be filed by 31 January 2009.

Following completion of the LLP return, the firm should provide each member with a member's statement showing their share of income as reported on that return. Each member is then responsible for including this income on his or her personal tax return.

3 SALARIED MEMBERS

7.3 The taxation and NIC position of salaried members of an LLP is complex and, at the time of writing, perhaps somewhat uncertain. Where a partner satisfies all of the normal badges of self-employment then they will be treated as self-employed. However, in addition, HMRC currently view all salaried members who are registered as members at Companies House as self-employed. However, the LLPA clearly allows for employee members which would imply that such salaried members are capable of being treated as an employee of the LLP. It is the view of the author of this chapter that if it is intended that salaried members are to be taxed as self-employed their arrangements should be capable of meeting the normal criteria of self-employment. Typically this would include the requirement for the members in question to provide capital to the LLP and participate in the variable profits of the business (and possibly losses to some degree).

Where members of an LLP are treated as partners, not employees, the self-employed (Class II and Class IV) rates of National Insurance will apply.

4 TIMING OF TAX PAYMENTS

7.4 Each member is required to settle his or her tax liability by making two payments on account and a final balancing payment. The payments on account fall due for payment on 31 January during the fiscal year and 31 July following the end of the fiscal year. Each payment on account is based upon 50 per cent of the previous year's income tax and Class IV National Insurance contributions liability. The final balancing payment falls due for payment on 31 January following the end of the fiscal year.

Example

For the fiscal year 2007/08 tax will fall due for payment as follows:

1st payment on account	31 January 2008
2nd payment on account	31 July 2008
Balancing payment	31 January 2009*

* The 1st payment on account in respect of the 2008/09 year will also be due for payment on this date.

Class IV National Insurance contributions are paid at the same time as the tax liability.

5 PROVIDING FOR TAX IN THE ACCOUNTS

7.5 There is no requirement for an LLP to make provision for tax in its accounts. However, many firms choose to set aside a separate tax reserve to ensure that members can pay their tax liabilities. There is no requirement to make separate disclosure of the tax reserves as the LLP is merely acting as agent on behalf of the members.

The basis of reserving for tax will differ depending upon factors such as the LLP's year end, working capital requirements and the general attitude of members to setting aside funds. It may however be appropriate to set aside funds which are sufficient to cover tax payments falling due over the course of the following 12 months. The timing of tax payments means that if profits fall, members can often find that they are paying tax on an earlier year's higher profits from the reduced current year drawings. It should be borne in mind that in the event that the firm is insolvent and required to pay out to creditors any tax reserves will form part of the members' funds available for distribution. However, the forecast tax liability may dissipate as a result of the availability of losses although some firms may prefer to keep their tax reserves outside of the LLP using a 'tax trust account'.

6 PROFITS SUBJECT TO TAX

7.6 The starting point for assessing taxable profits will be the profit as shown in the annual accounts. Since the tax year 1999/00 HMRC have required all 'self-employed' individuals (which includes members of LLPs and partners of partnerships) to prepare accounts for *tax purposes* on a Generally Accepted Accounting Practice (either UK GAAP or IFRS) basis. Unlike a partnership, an LLP is required to prepare accounts on this basis and therefore the taxable profits are more aligned to the accounting profits than may be the case for any predecessor partnerships.

The members of an LLP may agree to allocate to the members an amount which is different from the amount shown as profit or loss for the financial year available for division among members (see Chapter 5). For tax purposes, however, the members will be subject to tax on all profits arising regardless of whether the profits have been allocated to them or not. The total amount of profit, as adjusted for tax purposes (see below), is divided between the members in accordance with their arrangements for profit sharing, and it is this amount that is subject to tax. If the firm holds unallocated profits, a member may be subject to tax on a sum far greater than the amount he has actually received. The LLP will need to establish a mechanism to deal with this situation.

Whilst taxable profits will be based upon the profit shown in the accounts, tax legislation provides for certain adjustments to be made before the taxable profit can be established. For example, depreciation is not an allowable deduction for tax purposes, although relief is given for the purchase of some fixed assets by way of capital allowances.

Complications can arise where a LLP incurs a loss. As part of the firm's liability protection for members, many LLPs will have provisions which ensure that the loss is kept within the LLP and is not, for accounting and legal purposes, allocated to the members. However, when submitting the tax return for the LLP, it will be necessary to allocate the loss to members.

In the case of trading LLPs, losses may be restricted as a result of the HMRC Press Release dated 2 March 2007. At the time of writing, formal legislation has not been drafted, but the Press Release seeks to restrict the availability of losses for members who spend less than ten hours on average per week in the activities of the LLP. It is expected that legislation concerning this Press Release will be included in the 2007 Finance Act in due course.

7 RETIREMENT BENEFITS AND ANNUITIES

7.7 As discussed in Chapter 6, the SORP requires an LLP to provide for the present value of the best estimate of the expected liability for future payments to current and former members.

The amounts charged in the accounts can be significant. The tax legislation does not however recognise annuities as being an allowable expense from profits for tax purposes. Relief is given as a charge on income against each member's overall tax liability as and when the annuity is paid. Basic rate tax relief (22 per cent for 2007/08) is given at source on the payment of the annuity to the former member. If the members are higher rate taxpayers, they may then make a claim on their personal tax return for relief from the remainder of the tax. The amount of the annuity paid in the *fiscal year* is disclosed on the LLP return and on each member's statement. The member must declare the charge on income on the personal section of his tax return and not on the partnership pages relating to the LLP.

Whilst the members eventually receive full tax relief for the annuity, the relief is given over the life of the annuity rather than when a provision is made in the accounts.

8 OTHER PROVISIONS

7.8 Annuities are perhaps the exception to the general rule for allowing provisions for tax purposes. HMRC will generally allow a tax deduction to be claimed for provisions that are made in accordance with FRS 12.

9 MEMBERS' BORROWINGS

7.9 An LLP may borrow funds itself or require its members to contribute capital for which they may need to borrow funds from a bank. If the LLP borrows money any interest is likely to be allowable for tax purposes as an expense through the profit and loss account. Interest on members' loans will not be an expense in the profit and loss account, but members can, in general, obtain tax relief for the interest paid through their personal tax returns. However, an important exception to this rule is for members of investment LLPs and property investment LLPs where no relief is available on members' loans to provide capital.

Where capital is withdrawn from the LLP, this will be treated as reducing the amount of capital invested and therefore tax relief will not be available on the proportion of the loan interest relating to the withdrawn funds. In order to show a clear trail of capital invested in the LLP, it is recommended that separate records of capital and current accounts are maintained within the LLP so that profits can be withdrawn without affecting tax relief on borrowings for the firm's capital.

Where members have mortgages or other borrowings which do not attract any interest tax relief, it may be possible to arrange for the borrowing to be taken out in respect of LLP capital and therefore obtain tax relief. This is known as capital recycling and it is imperative that any recycling is carried out in a strict order and that the transactions are completed and are not mere book entries.

Care must be taken with any capital recycling, particularly in light of the case of *Lancaster v IRC* in which interest relief was denied on borrowing to fund a partnership. Advice from a specialist tax adviser should be sought to ensure that any recycling is not caught by this case.

10 CAPITAL GAINS TAX

7.10 The assets of an LLP are treated for tax purposes as owned by the members. Whilst members may own the assets in differing ratios to their normal profit sharing arrangements, in the absence of a separate agreement, any proceeds from the disposal of an asset would be taxed on the members in their normal profit sharing ratios.

The proceeds from the disposal of an asset must be reported on the LLP's tax return. However, the gain is only calculated on the capital gains tax pages of the member's tax return. Where the LLP is carrying on a trading activity, a gain arising on the disposal of an asset used in the firm's business will benefit from business asset taper relief. This reduces the taxable gain to 50 per cent of the total if the asset has been held for 12 months, and to just 25 per cent if the asset has been held for 24 months or more. In effect this reduces the rate of tax for a higher rate taxpayer to just 10 per cent where an asset has been held for more than two years.

In the case of a property investment LLP the rate of taper relief will depend on whether the asset was used wholly or partly for the purposes of a trade.

Where there has been a revaluation of the firm's assets, followed by a subsequent change in the asset sharing ratios, complications arise because each change in the asset sharing ratios amounts to a disposal by those members reducing their share of the asset and an acquisition by those increasing their share. This can require complex capital gains tax records to be maintained and the performance of involved computations.

It should be noted that where an LLP 'merges' with another business as discussed in Chapter 9, it is likely that such a merger will have to be accounted for as an acquisition. Where this is the case, goodwill of the acquired business may be included in the LLP's accounts. This will be treated the same as a revaluation of assets of the firm and trigger the need for detailed capital gains tax records to be maintained.

Chapter 8

Revenue recognition and work in progress

1 THE CONCEPT OF EARNED INCOME

8.1 The way in which service organisations including professional firms recognise income and work in progress has been subject to significant change in recent years. Prior to the issue of Application Note G (ANG) to Financial Reporting Standard 5: Reporting the substance of transactions (FRS 5), which took effect for accounting periods ending on or after 23 December 2003, there was no UK accounting standard that dealt explicitly with revenue recognition. Other than work that fell to be treated under the long-term accounting provisions of Statement of Standard Accounting Practice 9: Stocks and long-term contracts (SSAP 9), which are discussed further at **8.6**, many professional practices simply recognised income at the date a fee note was raised. To the extent work had been performed that had not been invoiced at the year end; this was usually recognised as work in progress.

However, ANG and the subsequent guidance on its application to service contracts, which was provided in Urgent Issues Task Force Abstract 40 (UITF 40) made it clear that income should be recognised when it had been earned by providing the related services, regardless of the timing of invoicing and payment.

2 THE PRINCIPLES OF REVENUE RECOGNITION FOR SERVICE CONTRACTS

8.2 The underlying principle of ANG and UITF 40 is that income on a service contract should be recognised when a business has earned the right to payment through performance of the underlying work. This principle is consistent with the long-term contract provisions of SSAP 9, which require turnover and, to the extent it is reasonably foreseeable, profit to be recognised as activity on a contract progresses. The definition of long-term contract in SSAP 9 covers two sets of circumstances; firstly, where a contract is of greater than one year's duration and, secondly, where a contract of less than one year's duration spans an accounting period and the effect on the financial statements is material. Whilst the former part of the definition was well understood the latter had frequently been interpreted as applying on an individual contract basis. UITF 40 clarified the position by stating that the long-term contract accounting requirements of SSAP 9 must also be applied where the aggregate effect of applying it across populations of similar contracts would be material.

To the extent therefore that a service organisation has performed work and the fee is not conditional on a future event outside the entity's control; this will normally represent earned income. As a result, unbilled amounts should be accrued at selling price and be recognised as revenue within the profit and loss account, rather than simply deferring the associated cost as work in progress to match against income in the future when an invoice is raised.

3 ANALYSING CONTRACTS

8.3 In determining the extent to which revenue needs to be recognised at the year end, the contracts in progress at the year end need to be analysed and their terms understood. Many contracts will stipulate when fees on account are to be raised but these may not correlate with the principles of revenue recognition. Some contracts, because of their size or complexity, may need to be considered individually. In other cases examination of a single contract may show it to have a number of individually identifiable phases and each of those phases may need to be accounted for separately. More commonly, however, there will be a number of contracts to provide a similar type of service which should be considered together.

In general, achieving the right to payment on a service contract will be related directly to performance. As such, revenue should ordinarily be recognised in proportion to the extent of progress on the contract. In most cases the extent of contract activity can be determined by comparing the amount of time spent on providing the service up to the date of the accounts to the total time that it is expected will be spent in delivering the service.

For example, consider the position of a tax accountant who is halfway through completing a client's tax return at the accountant's financial year end. Whilst it could be argued that a half-completed tax return is of little practical use, it can also be assumed that the computation will be completed and, by extension, that the accountant will complete all of the tax returns that he is working on at his year end. UITF 40 requires that the principles of SSAP 9 should be applied in accounting for this contract. The accountant would therefore recognise 50% of the income from the individual contract, and then apply similar calculations to all other contracts.

Not all contracts will be so straightforward and contract terms need to be examined carefully to identify specific circumstances, such as identifiable milestones or contingent fee arrangements, which affect how the associated revenue should be calculated.

Where a contract has identifiable milestones revenue will be recognised dependent on the milestones that have already been reached and the extent of progress towards the next milestone.

Where there is a contingent fee arrangement and the contingency is outside of the control of the reporting entity then no revenue should be recognised until the contingent event occurs. For example, where a barrister works on a 'no win, no fee' basis, the outcome of the trial will be outside the control of the barrister. Therefore he should not recognise any revenue until a case has been won, because it is only at that stage that the barrister has a right to consideration.

Even where the contingency is resolved after the financial period end, but before the accounts are approved, no revenue should be recognised in the period.

4 DETERMINING THE VALUE OF REVENUE

8.4 The value attributable to the recognised proportion of revenue under a service contract is determined with reference to how much can be charged for the work that is being performed. This will usually be stipulated in the contract either in the form of a lump sum amount, an hourly rate or a combination of the two.

Where fees are charged to the client with reference to time spent at an hourly rate, staff members are normally required to input details of how much time they have spent on different tasks and clients into a time recording system. In this situation, firms often calculate accrued income by starting with unbilled time as stated in their time recording systems, valued at standard hourly rates. This will then be adjusted for amounts that are not expected to be fully recoverable, either on a case-by-case basis, or by applying a percentage write-down that is reflective of the firm's normal under-recovery on charge rates.

For certain types of service, contracts may stipulate two different fees dependent upon the outcome of a future event. Revenue should only be recognised based on the value the entity is certain to get – usually the lowest.

For example, a lawyer has a contract to advise company A on the acquisition of company B. The fees agreed with company A are that if the transaction is successful the lawyer will bill £125,000 and if it is unsuccessful the fee will be £75,000. At the year end it is estimated that 60% of the services have been provided, the appropriate level of revenue to be included in the accounts would be £45,000 (60% of £75.000).

5 ACCOUNTING ENTRIES

8.5 Where an entity recognises revenue in respect of work that has been performed but not yet billed, this amount is included in turnover and also as accrued income within debtors. Alternatively, some professional practices have chosen to disclose the accrued income using the SSAP 9 terminology, 'amounts recoverable on contracts'. The cost of performing the work should not be carried forward within work in progress, but should be recognised as a cost in the profit and loss account.

Where invoices have been raised which exceed the amount of revenue that can be recognised, then these should not be included in the profit and loss account but as deferred income within creditors. If the amounts have been paid, then they should be disclosed within creditors as 'payments received on account'.

6 WORK IN PROGRESS

8.6 Where an entity has carried out work but has not yet met the criteria to recognise revenue, for example, if work has been performed where the ability to charge the client is contingent upon a future event, work in progress may still be recognised.

Work in progress is an example of the 'matching' concept of accounting. If costs have been incurred to produce goods or services in one period and the related revenue will not arise until a later period, then the costs are deferred and released in the period that the revenue arises. Costs should only be deferred to the extent that they are expected to be recovered against future revenue and so work in progress is recognised at the lower of cost and net realisable value (ie the amount that will be received net of any further costs to be incurred in the process).

If the future income to which work in progress relates is contingent upon a conditional event (eg a success fee on completion of a transaction), it is not until the contingency settles that the LLP is able to establish the net realisable value of the year-end work in progress. If the contingency subsequently settles and the success fee is earned, this would support the inclusion of work in progress performed prior to the balance sheet date at cost, but, where the contingency remains unsettled, work in progress would normally be written down to nil value, on the basis that the potential net realisable value is nil.

In theory, the period up to the date when the accounts are signed should be considered in determining the appropriate value for work in progress, but this leaves profit open to manipulation by extending or reducing the post balance sheet period. Therefore, in practice, most LLPs will set a defined post balance sheet period, for example, if a contingent fee has not been earned within three months of the balance sheet date, full provision will be made against the carrying value of the associated work in progress.

7 DETERMINING THE COST OF WORK IN PROGRESS

8.7 As noted at **8.6**, accounting standards require that work in progress be included in the balance sheet at the lower of cost and net realisable value. SSAP 9 defines cost to include not only materials (unlikely to be relevant to the majority of LLPs) but also direct labour and overheads.

Direct labour should include the cost of those employees who have been directly involved in the provision of the related service. The employees' cost should include not only their wages or salaries, but also other employment costs such as National Insurance and pensions. Where members' time is included within work in progress it should be valued to the extent that it is charged as an expense in the profit and loss account (see Chapter 5). Amounts received by members by way of allocation of profits available for division amongst members should be excluded from the valuation of work in progress.

SSAP 9 requires that all 'direct' overheads should be included within the valuation of work in progress. Other overheads should only be included in work in progress where this is justified by exceptional circumstances: those which are properly classified as selling or administrative overheads should not be included.

Overheads should be allocated to work in progress on the basis of the LLP's normal level of activity. Overhead costs which are the result of inefficiencies, such as the effect of abnormal changes in procedures, should not be included in the valuation.

Irrespective of whether the time input by a member is included within work in progress, the general accounting requirement to match costs and revenues means that any overhead related to the member's time should be included in the valuation.

The above principles will also apply to any stock produced by an LLP involved in manufacturing or production.

8 VALUING WORK IN PROGRESS IN PRACTICE

8.8 In calculating the cost of work in progress, some professional services firms take the value of unbilled fee-earner time at charge rates as a starting point and then reduce this value by the gross profit element included within the charge rates. Others build up an hourly cost for each fee-earner from their salary and related costs plus an allocation of overheads.

Whichever method is used, the firm will need to determine the amount of overheads to be included in work in progress (or to be deducted in arriving at gross profit). Particular problems may arise when trying to deal with areas such as central management overheads. Salaries for this area may well include an element of either direct provision of service or the supervision of service delivery, as well as administration. Central costs should be apportioned between direct and indirect costs on a reasonable basis and this should then be consistently applied.

Where an hourly cost is calculated for each fee-earner, further complications can arise in allocating the overheads between fee-earners. The most usual approach is an allocation which is in proportion to direct labour costs.

In practice, a complicated method of calculating the cost of work in progress is often unnecessary, and a simple method, which can be justified as reasonable and is consistently applied, should normally be adequate.

For most firms, a significant part of the standard 'selling price' relates to recovery of indirect costs and profit and the cost of work in progress may be in the region of 30–40% of its value at selling price. As a result, unless the work is subject to an unsettled contingency, which will potentially cause it to be heavily discounted, or no charge to be made for it, it is relatively unusual for further provision against the cost of work in progress to be necessary.

Chapter 9

Business combinations

1 INTRODUCTION

9.1 This chapter looks at the accounting consequences of an LLP acquiring another business either by taking a direct investment (equity, partnership share, etc) or by acquiring the assets, liabilities and trade without making a direct investment in the disposing entity. In these circumstances there are accounting implications both for the LLP's accounts and for group accounts where the LLP is required to prepare them (see Chapter 2 for the exemptions from the requirement to prepare group accounts).

2 GENERAL ACCOUNTING PRINCIPLES FOR BUSINESS COMBINATIONS

9.2 There are currently two possible methods of accounting for a business combination within consolidated accounts—acquisition accounting or merger accounting. The conditions which must be met before merger accounting can be applied are discussed below, but the rules contained within accounting standards are extremely strict and as a result mergers in the corporate environment are relatively rare. The strict criteria for merger accounting are particularly relevant to those partnerships transferring to LLP status as historically most partnerships have regarded their business combinations as mergers, but a large number of these would not meet the accounting requirements and fall to be treated as acquisitions.

In addition to the requirements set out in legislation, accounting for business combinations is also governed by a number of accounting standards:

- FRS 2—'Accounting for subsidiary undertakings'
- FRS 6—'Acquisitions and mergers'
- FRS 7—'Fair values in acquisition accounting'
- FRS 10—'Goodwill and intangible assets'

3 PRINCIPLES OF ACQUISITION ACCOUNTING

9.3 The general principle of consolidated accounts is that they should present the financial position and results of the parent and its subsidiary undertakings as if they were a single LLP. Under acquisition accounting, when the group acquires a new subsidiary, the parent LLP is treated as having acquired the assets and liabilities at their 'fair value' at the date of acquisition and the income and expenditure of the subsidiary is only included in the consolidated profit and loss account from the date of acquisition.

In preparing the consolidation, the cost of the investment in the subsidiary shown on the balance sheet of the parent LLP will nearly always differ from the fair value of the assets and liabilities of the subsidiary at the date of acquisition. The difference between the aggregate fair values of the assets and liabilities and the purchase consideration (cost of investment) represents either positive or negative goodwill, the accounting treatment of which is discussed at **9.9**.

4 DETERMINING THE DATE OF ACQUISITION

9.4 The date of acquisition determines the extent to which the profits or losses of the acquired business are included in the group accounts. FRS 2 sets out the rules for determining the date of acquisition of a subsidiary and this should be the date on which control passes to the LLP. The date that control passes is a matter of fact and it cannot be artificially altered, for example by including within the purchase and sale agreement some other 'effective' date.

FRS 2 states that:

> 'the date on which the consideration for the transfer of control is paid is often an important indication of the date on which a subsidiary undertaking is acquired or disposed of. However, the date the consideration passes is not conclusive evidence of the date of the transfer of control because this date can be set to fall on a date other than that on which control is transferred, with compensation for any lead or lag included in the consideration. Consideration may also be paid in instalments.'

Where there is an earn-out arrangement, or consideration is payable in instalments, the date of acquisition is not usually deferred, and all the circumstances should be considered in order to determine when control passes. It can, however, usually be assumed that control passes on the date on which an offer to purchase becomes unconditional.

5 COST OF ACQUISITION

9.5 The cost of an acquisition is the aggregate of:

- the amount of cash paid;
- the fair value of any other purchase consideration given by the acquirer; and
- the expenses of the acquisition.

The cost of acquisition will also determine the carrying value of the investment on the balance sheet of the LLP.

The fair value of purchase consideration is determined by reference to the following:

- *Cash and other monetary items* (for example, monetary assets given or liabilities assumed). The amount paid or payable.
- *Interest in the LLP.* Where there has been a recent valuation of the LLP it may be possible to value the consideration by reference to such a valuation. However, both FRS 7 and the SORP acknowledge that for any type of entity in which there is no ready market for its securities or other interests, the best estimate of value may be obtained by valuing the acquired entity.
- *Non-monetary consideration.* Estimated by reference to market prices, estimated realisable values, independent valuations or other available evidence.

It is not unusual for an acquisition agreement to provide for part of the purchase consideration to be deferred to a future date (deferred consideration) or to be contingent upon the occurrence of some future event (contingent consideration). FRS 7 specifically requires the cost of acquisition to include the fair value of deferred consideration which can be calculated by discounting the estimated amounts of cash that will be paid to their present values using the rate at which the LLP could obtain similar borrowings. FRS 7 also requires the cost of acquisition to include a reasonable estimate of the fair value of the amounts of contingent consideration expected to be payable in the future. Where necessary, the estimates should be reviewed and adjusted at each balance sheet date subsequent to acquisition, with a consequent amendment to goodwill.

9.6 In considering accounting for an acquisition by an LLP, reference should be had not only to those parts of the agreement that deal with the consideration, but also those dealing with the arrangements entered into for profit sharing with new members. These may also include an element of contingent consideration. For example, the members of the acquired entity might be awarded an increased profit share for a limited period after the acquisition, which subsequently reduces back to a 'normal' level. In these circumstances it will be necessary for the LLP to make an estimate of the future profits which will be earned and to include an estimate of the enhanced members' interests as part of the acquisition cost.

Deferred or contingent consideration should be included in the balance sheet as a liability at the time of acquisition. The most appropriate position will usually be within 'Provisions for liabilities'.

Where the deferred or contingent consideration is to be satisfied by an enhanced profit share, rather than include the amount within provisions it should be shown as part of members' other interests preferably under a separate heading such as 'Members' interests in respect of deferred consideration'. As the conditions for the increased membership are reached transfers should be made to capital accounts or debt due to members dependent on the terms agreed with the new members.

The cost of acquisition should also include any associated expenses. FRS 7 limits the amount that can be included to those costs which have been incurred directly in making the acquisition. The expenses should not include any allocation of costs that would have been incurred irrespective of whether or not the acquisition had been entered into, for example management remuneration.

6 DETERMINING THE FAIR VALUE OF ASSETS AND LIABILITIES

9.7 The assets and liabilities to be included in the assessment of fair value are all those which existed at the date of acquisition. In determining fair value the following should be taken into account:

- the conditions in existence at the date of acquisition;
- fair value should not reflect any changes resulting from the LLP's intentions or actions taken subsequent to the date of acquisition;
- fair value should not reflect any impairment, or other changes, resulting from events subsequent to the acquisition;
- provisions or accruals for future operating losses should not be included;
- no provisions or accruals should be made for reorganisation and integration costs expected to be incurred, whether relating to the acquired entity or the LLP.

Fair value should be assessed by reference to the LLP's accounting policies. Therefore, where accounting policies differ between the LLP and the entity acquired the values of the assets and liabilities should be adjusted to bring them into line with the LLP's accounting policies.

The general requirement within FRS 7 is that the fair value exercise should be completed, if possible, by the date on which the first accounts including the acquired business are approved by the members. This may not always be possible, particularly where the date of acquisition is close to the year end. In these circumstances provisional valuations should be made, which should be amended, if necessary, in the next accounts with a corresponding adjustment to goodwill. The accounts for the first year post acquisition should make it clear that the fair values are provisional. Adjustments beyond this period must be charged to the profit and loss account.

It is not unusual for purchase and sale agreements to include values for the assets and liabilities of the acquired business. These may however differ from the fair values and reference should still be made to the provisions of FRS 7. The general principles for determining the fair values of different classes of assets and liabilities are set out below:

- *Tangible fixed assets.* The lower of the recoverable amount and depreciated replacement cost. Where similar assets are bought and sold on the open market (for example, property), the value can be determined by reference to market value.
- *Intangible fixed assets.* These must be capable of being valued separately to the underlying business before they can be recognised. The fair value should be determined by reference to replacement cost, which will usually be market value.
- *Stocks and work in progress.* Lower of replacement cost or net realisable value. Replacement cost is the cost at which the stocks would have been replaced by the acquired entity, reflecting its normal buying process and the sources of supply and prices available to it. Current cost would include members' time as discussed in Chapter 8.
- *Quoted investments.* Market price (adjusted if necessary for unusual price fluctuations or for the size of holding).
- *Monetary assets and liabilities.* The fair value should take into account the amounts expected to be paid or received.
- *Contingent assets and liabilities.* Contingent assets and liabilities should only be included if the contingency existed at the date of acquisition. The value should be based on a reasonable estimate of expected outcome.
- *Businesses sold or acquired exclusively with a view to subsequent resale.* Where a purchaser has been identified or is being sought and the

disposal is reasonably expected to occur within approximately one year of the date of the acquisition, the operation should be valued at an estimate of the sales proceeds. Such items should be included as a single asset within current assets.

- *Pensions and other post-retirement benefits.* For a funded scheme, the amount of the surplus or deficiency should be recognised as an asset or liability respectively. An asset should, however, only be recognised to the extent that it can be recovered through reduced contributions or through refunds from the scheme. For unfunded schemes the valuation of accrued obligations should be recognised as a liability.

7 ACQUISITION OF A BUSINESS

9.8 Similar accounting provisions will apply where an LLP acquires the assets and liabilities of a business rather than making an investment therein. The principal difference is that any goodwill arising will be recorded on the LLP's own balance sheet instead of only on the consolidated balance sheet. In these circumstances amortisation of goodwill will be charged against, and directly affect, the profits of the LLP available for distribution to the members.

8 GOODWILL

9.9 A successful business will be worth more than the sum of its net assets and therefore has 'goodwill'. Accounting standards do not permit such 'internally generated goodwill' to be included on the balance sheet; it may only be included to the extent that it was acquired for 'valuable consideration'. The acquisition of a business provides an indication of the level of goodwill and valuable consideration is provided by the purchase consideration, accordingly purchased goodwill has to be included on the balance sheet.

A number of partnerships include goodwill on their balance sheet. In some circumstances this arises not as a result of the purchase of another business, but for example as part of a revaluation exercise to calculate the cost of capital for new partners. Such goodwill does not represent purchased goodwill as defined within accounting standards and as a result cannot be recognised on transition to an LLP.

Goodwill is usually considered to have a limited useful economic life and FRS 10 requires that it be amortised over that period. FRS 10 contains a presumption that the useful economic life of goodwill is 20 years or less. That presumption may be rebutted and either a longer life or an indefinite life may be substituted, provided both of the following conditions are met:

- the durability of the acquired business can be demonstrated and justifies estimating the useful economic life to exceed 20 years; and
- the goodwill is capable of continued measurement (so that annual impairment reviews will be feasible).

Whilst a number of companies have chosen to amortise goodwill over 20 years in order to take advantage of the maximum period before impairment testing is required, this period should only be applied if it genuinely reflects the position of the acquired business. In a number of industries a life shorter or longer than 20 years will be appropriate.

If, in exceptional circumstances, it is considered that goodwill has an indefinite useful economic life, it should not be amortised.

In rare circumstances the cost of acquisition may be less than the fair value of the assets and liabilities acquired. In such cases 'negative goodwill' arises. FRS 10 requires that there is firstly a reassessment of the fair values to ensure that assets are not overstated and liabilities omitted. Once the LLP is satisfied that there has been a genuine 'bargain purchase' the negative goodwill is included on the balance sheet as a negative intangible asset and it is amortised in line firstly with the consumption of non-monetary assets (eg tangible fixed assets) and secondly over the period the members consider the LLP will benefit from the acquisition.

9 IMPAIRMENT TESTING OF GOODWILL

9.10 Goodwill which is considered to have a life that is either indefinite or in excess of 20 years is required to have a review for impairment at the end of every reporting period. In addition, FRS 10 requires that goodwill which is being amortised over 20 years or less should be subject to impairment reviews in the following circumstances:

- A 'first-year review'—a review at the end of the first full financial year following acquisition.
- A review at the end of any period when events or changes of circumstances indicate that the carrying value may not be recoverable.

The requirements in relation to impairment testing are set out in FRS 11 'Impairment of fixed assets and goodwill' and are potentially both difficult to perform and time-consuming and usually involve the preparation of discounted cash flow calculations based on future projections of earnings.

Whilst the requirements with respect to impairment reviews are generally quite onerous, FRS 10 permits the mandatory first-year review to be performed in two stages:

- by comparing the first year's performance after acquisition with pre-acquisition forecasts used to support the purchase price; and then
- by carrying out a full impairment review only if either the results of the first stage indicate a shortfall from expectations or if any other previously unforeseen events or changes in circumstances indicate that the carrying values may not be recoverable.

10 APPLICATION OF MERGER ACCOUNTING

9.11 FRS 6, which is written in the context of companies, defines a merger as 'a business combination that results in the creation of a new reporting entity formed from the combining parties, in which the shareholders of the combining entities come together in partnership for the mutual sharing of the risks and benefits of the combined entity, and in which no party to the combination in substance obtains control over any other, or is otherwise seen to be dominant, whether by virtue of the proportion of its shareholders' rights in the combined entity, the influence of its directors or otherwise'.

When there is a 'true' merger (see **9.12**), FRS 6 requires merger accounting to be used. Merger accounting may also be used when there is a business combination which meets the definition of a group reconstruction. Whilst FRS 6 does not make merger accounting mandatory in the latter case, it is generally considered that merger accounting as opposed to acquisition accounting should be applied to group reconstructions in order for the accounts to give a true and fair view.

Considerations relating to transition from a partnership to an LLP are dealt with in more detail in Chapter 14. However, in general, these should be accounted for as group reconstructions using merger accounting.

11 CONDITIONS PERMITTING MERGER ACCOUNTING

9.12 Unlike the legislation applicable to companies which sets out criteria that have to be met for merger accounting to apply – the primary concern being levels of share capital issued and acquired – CA 85 as applied to LLPs states that 'the conditions for accounting for an acquisition as a merger are that adoption of the merger method of accounting accords with generally accepted accounting principles or practice'. This therefore requires consideration of the five criteria of FRS 6 which have to be met before merger accounting applies. These are set out below.

A Role of each party

9.13 This requires an assessment of the way the roles of each party to the combination are portrayed and, in particular, whether either party is portrayed as either acquirer or acquired. This will often be a very subjective assessment and one which will depend both upon the actual behaviour of the management of each of the combining parties and perceptions of that behaviour. One factor that could be considered is the relative benefits obtained by each of the parties to the transaction. If one party is clearly obtaining benefits that are substantially greater than the other (for example, disproportionate profit shares) then it should not be regarded as a merger. FRS 6 also states that the circumstances surrounding the transaction should be examined. The following are factors to consider:

- the form by which the combination was achieved;
- the plans for the combined entity's future operations (for example, whether any closures or disposals affect one party more than the other);
- the proposed corporate image (such as the name, logo and the location of the headquarters and principal operations); and
- the way in which the transaction has been portrayed in any external communication.

B Involvement in management

9.14 The role taken by each party in the selection of the management of the combined LLP must also be considered. All parties to the combination should be involved in establishing the management structure for the combined entity and in selecting the management personnel. The decisions should be seen to be made on the basis of a consensus between the parties to the combination rather than purely by exercise of voting rights. This does not preclude the possibility that all, or most, of the management team of the combined entity comes from only one of the parties, provided that this clearly reflects the wishes of the others. The considerations should go beyond the formal management structure and take into account all those involved in the main financial and operating decisions and the way in which the decision-making process operates in practice post-combination.

C The relative sizes of each party

9.15 The guidance in FRS 6 is based on a corporate model and contains a presumption that one party will dominate if it is more than 50 per cent larger than each of the other parties to the combination, judged by reference to the ownership interests – meaning the proportion of the equity of the combined entity attributable to the shareholders of each of the combining parties. The SORP, in acknowledging that this criterion may be difficult to interpret in the circumstances of LLPs, suggests alternatives which may be more appropriate. These alternatives include consideration of the levels of revenue, number of members, profits and employees. The exact nature of the combination should also be considered in order to establish whether it might be appropriate to rebut the 50 per cent limit.

D Form of consideration

9.16 It is necessary to establish whether the form of consideration includes any payment other than an interest in the LLP. Under the terms of the combination or related arrangements, the consideration received by the members of each party to the combination, in relation to their interests, should be primarily capital in the combined LLP; and any other form of consideration (most usually cash), or capital with reduced voting or distribution rights, should be an immaterial proportion of the fair value of the total consideration.

E Interest in combined business

9.17 The issue in this instance is whether the members of the combined entity retain an interest in the performance of only part of it. Any form of earn-out arrangement contained within the purchase and sale agreement will result in this criterion not being met. The existence of an arrangement whereby the allocation of consideration to the combining parties depends on the determination of the eventual value of a specific liability or asset contributed by one of the parties would not, however, automatically invalidate this criterion, although the specific circumstances would need to be addressed.

12 THE ACCOUNTING CONSEQUENCES OF A MERGER

9.18 Where all of the criteria for merger accounting are met the accounting in the consolidated accounts is as follows. The net assets of the two entities are combined using their existing book values – no fair value adjustments are required. Adjustments will, however, need to be made as necessary to ensure that the same accounting policies are applied. No goodwill or negative goodwill will be recognised. The consolidated profit and loss account will include the profits of each entity for the entire period, regardless of the date of the merger, and the comparative amounts in the consolidated accounts should be restated to the aggregate of the amounts recorded by the two entities in the previous period.

13 EFFECT OF POSSIBLE HARMONISATION WITH INTERNATIONAL FINANCIAL REPORTING STANDARDS

9.19 IFRS 3 'Business combinations' has a different approach to accounting for business combinations and goodwill:

- Merger accounting is not permitted and an acquirer must always be identified in any business combination.
- Goodwill cannot be amortised and instead is subject to annual impairment review.
- Negative goodwill is not recognised on the balance sheet, and any excess of assets acquired over consideration is taken directly to income.

Chapter 10

Provisions

1 USE OF 'PROVISIONS'

10.1 In accountancy the term 'provision' can be used in two separate sets of circumstances. First, it refers to adjustments which are made to the amounts at which certain assets are included within the accounts. For example, 'Provision for bad or doubtful debts' or 'Provision for obsolete stock'. These are however accounting adjustments and are not strictly provisions at all. Secondly, and more importantly, this term is reserved for those items which can be included on the balance sheet within the heading 'Provisions for liabilities'. The accounting rules with respect to the recognition of such provisions are extremely strict and are set out in FRS 12 'Provisions, contingent liabilities and contingent assets'.

2 THE PRINCIPLES OF FRS 12

10.2 One of the reasons for issuing FRS 12 was to prevent reporting entities from smoothing their results by the creation of round sum provisions to take account of events that might happen in the future. For example, it was not uncommon for retail chains to make provisions for future shop refurbishment programmes and then release 'unused' elements of the provision in later periods.

Before an LLP can recognise a provision within its accounts it must be able to satisfy each of the three criteria set out in FRS 12:

- there must be a legal or constructive obligation at the balance sheet date as a result of an event occurring before that date;
- it must be probable that there will be a 'transfer of economic benefits' (for example, paying cash) to settle the obligation; and
- a reliable estimate can be made of the amount involved.

A constructive obligation arises where through custom and practice the LLP has created a valid expectation on the part of a third party that its claim will be met.

Where the obligation to pay only becomes apparent after the balance sheet date, but it clearly arises as the result of an event before that date, a provision should be recognised. For example, an unexpected legal claim might be received after the balance sheet date in respect of damage alleged to have occurred before that date. In these circumstances a provision would be recognised, but it would not be acceptable to create a general provision for possible legal claims arising from work performed. The latter has historically been an approach adopted particularly by professional practices to take account of potential professional indemnity claims. Such provisions are not permitted in the accounts of the LLP, but the members could decide to make an allowance for such possible claims prior to determining the profits available for distribution.

3 REPAIRS AND MAINTENANCE EXPENDITURE

10.3 Future repairs and maintenance do not relate to present obligations of the LLP arising as a result of a past event. Accordingly no provision should be made for them, even in the circumstances where legislation requires regular maintenance in order for the asset to continue to be used in the business. FRS 12 argues that there are no grounds for recognising a provision for future repairs and maintenance expenditure, because the costs relate to the future operation of the business. The one exception to this general rule is where an asset is held under a lease and the lease term includes a requirement for the asset to be made good at whatever stage of the lease it is returned to the lessor. In these circumstances there is both a legal obligation and a past event (the signing of the lease). Such terms are particularly common in the case of property leases where provision is often required for the future cost of dilapidations.

4 FUTURE OPERATING LOSSES

10.4 FRS 12 prohibits the recognition of the potential impact of future operating losses by means of:

- A general prohibition where there is no present obligation and thus no liability.
- A specific prohibition in respect of future operating losses incurred up to the date of a restructuring, unless the losses relate to an onerous contract (see **10.5**).

In both of these cases, the future losses relate to the continuing business. The situation is, however, different where a decision has been made to sell or terminate a business. FRS 3 'Reporting financial performance' which covers the accounting requirements for discontinued businesses states:

> If a decision has been made to sell or terminate an operation, any consequential provisions should reflect the extent to which obligations have been incurred that are not expected to be covered by the future profits of the operation. This principle requires that the reporting entity should be demonstrably committed to the sale or termination. The provision should cover only (a) the direct costs of the sale or termination and (b) any operating losses of the operation up to the date of sale or termination, in both cases, after taking into account the aggregate profit, if any, to be recognised in the profit and loss account from the future profits of the operation.

In these limited circumstances it is therefore possible to make provision for future operating losses.

5 ONEROUS CONTRACTS

10.5 An onerous contract is defined by FRS 12 as one '... in which the unavoidable costs of meeting the obligations under it exceed the economic benefits expected to be received under it'. Provision should be made for the obligations under such a contract. Provision should not, however, be made where the contract has merely turned out to be less profitable than originally envisaged. In these circumstances the effect on the carrying value of other related assets might however need to be considered.

One of the most common types of onerous contract is the lease on a vacated property. In these cases provision should be made in the accounts calculated by reference to the likely future rentals to be paid less any rent that can be obtained from subletting the property. The provision should also include the other costs associated with the property such as rates.

6 RESTRUCTURING COSTS

10.6 FRS 12 permits the recognition of a provision for the costs of restructuring in certain circumstances. The definition of restructuring is fairly widely drawn and includes:

- Sale or termination of a line of business.
- The closure of business locations in a country or region or the relocation of business activities from one country or region to another.

- Changes in management structure, for example eliminating a layer of management.
- Fundamental reorganisations that have a material effect on the nature and focus of the entity's operations.

In order for an LLP to be able to recognise a provision in respect of restructuring it must have both a detailed plan and a valid expectation that the plan will be implemented.

As a minimum the plan is required to specify the following:

- The business or part of business concerned.
- The principal locations affected.
- The location, function, and approximate number of employees who will be compensated for terminating their services.
- The amount of expenditure involved.
- When the plan will be implemented.

The decision by the members to go ahead with their plan will not, of itself, be sufficient to constitute a constructive obligation, there must be a valid expectation on the part of those affected that it will take place. This will be indicated either by the LLP having started to implement the plan or by having announced its main features to those who are affected by it.

The amounts which may be included within a restructuring provision are restricted to the direct expenditure arising from the restructuring, which is both necessarily entailed by the restructuring and not associated with the ongoing activities of the entity. The following items are specifically excluded by FRS 12:

- Retraining or relocating continuing staff.
- Marketing.
- Investment in new systems and distribution networks.

7 REIMBURSEMENT OF AMOUNTS INCLUDED WITHIN PROVISIONS

10.7 In certain circumstances the risk reflected by the provision might be offset by arrangements for reimbursement, for example through an insurance policy. The reimbursement may be recognised in the accounts when it is virtually certain that it will be received upon the settlement of the provision. The reimbursement should, however, be recognised in the balance sheet as a separate asset and not offset against the related liability. In the profit and loss account, however, the expected income should be netted against the charge arising as a consequence of the provision.

Chapter 11

Related parties

1 THE SOURCE OF DISCLOSURE REQUIREMENTS

11.1 CA 1985 contains specific legislation and disclosure requirements aimed at preventing directors from taking financial advantage from their position. The special relationship that exists between members and an LLP means that none of this is reproduced in the LLPA. The only disclosure requirements contained within the LLPA are those which deal generally with members' interests (see Chapter 5).

LLPs do, however, have to comply with the full and more onerous requirements of FRS 8 'Related party disclosures'.

2 THE GENERAL REQUIREMENTS OF FRS 8

11.2 The objective of FRS 8 is 'to ensure that financial statements contain the disclosures necessary to draw attention to the possibility that the reported financial position and results may have been affected by the existence of related parties and by material transactions with them'. The FRS requires disclosure of a material transaction undertaken by the LLP with a related party, irrespective of whether a price is charged. Where the LLP is controlled by another party, disclosure is required of that controlling party, irrespective of whether any transactions have taken place with it.

3 IDENTIFYING RELATED PARTIES

11.3 FRS 8 defines two or more parties as being related when at any time during the financial period:

- one party had either direct or indirect control of the other party; or
- the parties were subject to common control from the same source; or

- one party had influence over the financial and operating policies of the other party to an extent that that other party might be inhibited from pursuing at all times its own separate interests; or
- the parties, in entering into a transaction, were subject to influence from the same source to such an extent that one of the parties to the transaction subordinated its own separate interests.

Certain parties are deemed to be related:

- The LLP's ultimate and intermediate parent undertakings, subsidiary undertakings and fellow subsidiary undertakings.
- The LLP's associates and joint ventures.
- The investor or venturer in respect of which the LLP is an associate or a joint venture.
- The directors of ultimate and intermediate parent companies.
- Pension funds for the benefit of employees of the LLP or of any entity that is a related party of it.
- Predecessor partnerships of the LLP.

Certain further parties are presumed to be related, unless it can be proven that neither party had influenced the financial outcome of a transaction:

- The key management of the LLP and the key management of its parent undertaking or undertakings (key management are those persons in senior positions having authority or responsibility for directing or controlling major activities and resources).
- An entity managing or managed by the LLP under a management contract.
- Members of the close family of any of the above individuals.
- Partnerships, companies, trusts and other entities in which any individual or member of the close family of the above has a controlling interest.

FRS 8 also includes the presumption that the directors of a company are related parties. This presumption should not be interpreted to mean that all members of an LLP are to be automatically regarded as related parties. Whether the members are related will depend upon the degree of control they have over the day-to-day activities of the LLP. In a small LLP it may be the case that all the members are directly involved in its management and as such should be regarded as related. However in a large LLP management may be devolved to a small number of members who should be presumed to be related, whereas the remainder will probably fall outside of the definition. The reference to key management in FRS 8 means that designated members will usually be related parties.

The fact that some members of an LLP are also members of another LLP is not of itself sufficient to make the two entities related. The extent to which they have control of both LLPs and are in a position to influence transactions between them will have to be considered.

The definition of close family in FRS 8 is much more far-reaching than that contained in CA 85. Close members of the family of an individual are those family members, or members of the same household, who may be expected to influence, or be influenced by, that person in their dealings with the LLP.

4 IDENTIFYING RELATED PARTY TRANSACTIONS

11.4 FRS 8 defines a related party transaction as 'the transfer of assets or liabilities or the performance of services by, or for a related party irrespective of whether a price is charged'. There is no exemption from disclosure simply because transactions are in the normal course of the LLP's business or at arm's length.

5 EXEMPTIONS FROM DISCLOSURE

11.5 There are some exemptions from disclosure and these are set out below:

- In consolidated accounts—transactions or balances between group members that have been eliminated on consolidation.
- Pension contributions paid to a pension fund. There are however significant disclosure requirements in respect of pension schemes arising from other accounting standards (see Chapter 6).
- Emoluments in respect of services as an employee.
- In a parent LLP's own accounts when they are presented together with its consolidated accounts.
- In the accounts of a subsidiary LLP, where 90 per cent or more of its voting rights are controlled within the group, of transactions with entities that are part of the group or investees of the group qualifying as related parties, provided that the consolidated financial statements in which the subsidiary LLP is included are publicly available and this fact is stated in the accounts.

6 CIRCUMSTANCES WHERE DISCLOSURE IS NOT REQUIRED

11.6 FRS 8 does not require disclosure of the relationship and transactions between the LLP and certain third parties which arise simply as a result of the normal role of those other parties. These include:

- Providers of finance in the course of business.
- Utility companies.
- Government departments and their sponsored bodies, even though they may circumscribe the freedom of action of an entity or participate in its decision-making process.
- A customer, supplier, franchiser, distributor or general agent with whom an entity transacts a significant volume of business.

7 MATERIALITY IN THE CONTEXT OF FRS 8

11.7 FRS 8 requires different considerations of materiality to that used by other accounting standards. Materiality should be judged not only in terms of the significance of the related party transaction to the LLP, but also in relation to the other related party when that party is:

- A designated member, key manager or other individual in a position to influence, or accountable for stewardship of, the LLP.
- A member of the close family of any such individual.
- An entity controlled by any individual referred to above.

The need to have reference to both parties to the transaction can result in transactions being disclosed which would not be if reference were made only to materiality in the context of the LLP.

8 INFORMATION THAT SHOULD BE DISCLOSED

11.8 For each related party transaction the following should be disclosed:

- The name of the related party.
- A description of the relationship between the LLP and the other party.
- A description of the transaction.

- The amounts involved.
- Any other elements of the transaction necessary for an understanding of the financial statements.
- The amounts due to or from related parties at the balance sheet date and any provision for doubtful debts due from such parties at that date.
- Amounts written off in the period in respect of debts due to or from related parties.

It is permitted to disclose transactions with related parties on an aggregated basis (aggregation of similar transactions by type of related party), unless disclosure of an individual transaction, or connected transactions, is necessary for an understanding of its impact on the accounts. Aggregation should not however be done in such a way as to obscure the importance of significant transactions. For example, purchases or sales of goods should not be aggregated with purchases or sales of fixed assets.

Comparative information should also be presented.

Chapter 12

Going concern

1 THE GOING CONCERN CONCEPT

12.1 Going concern is one of the fundamental principles underlying the preparation of the accounts of all entities. Accordingly, the majority of LLP accounts will be prepared on the basis that the LLP will continue in operational existence for the foreseeable future, known as the 'going concern basis'. The LLPA states that an LLP is presumed to be carrying on business as a going concern unless the accounts say otherwise. Application of FRS 18 'Accounting policies' also requires that an LLP should prepare its accounts on the going concern basis, unless the LLP is being liquidated or has ceased trading, or the members have no realistic alternative but to liquidate the LLP or to cease trading. In these circumstances it may be appropriate to prepare the accounts on a 'break up' basis.

In preparing the accounts the members will need to carry out such procedures as they consider necessary to satisfy themselves as to whether the going concern basis is appropriate. There may be factors about the business which cast doubts as to the going concern status of the LLP, for example the renegotiation of necessary bank facilities. In these circumstances the members will need to consider the actions that can be taken to mitigate those concerns. Disclosure of both the concerns and the mitigating action is required in the accounts in support of the members' view that it is appropriate to prepare the accounts on the going concern basis and that this results in the accounts giving a true and fair view of the position of the LLP.

Where there is concern about the ability of the LLP to continue as a going concern and the accounts do not include sufficient disclosure, the accounts may not give a true and fair view and this will be considered by the auditors who, as a consequence, may qualify their audit opinion.

FRS 18 deals with the going concern concept in detail and regards it as pervasive in the setting of accounting policies.

2 EVIDENCE SUPPORTING GOING CONCERN ASSESSMENTS

12.2 FRS 18 requires that, when preparing accounts, the members should assess whether there are significant doubts about the LLP's ability to continue as a going concern. This assessment is required to be made for what is termed the 'foreseeable future'. This should be a minimum of 12 months from the date on which the accounts are approved. If the foreseeable future considered by the members is less than one year from the date of approval of the accounts, the accounts are required to disclose this fact.

The extent of evidence required to support the members' assessment of going concern will be dependent on a number of factors. These include:

- The extent to which the LLP's financial resources exceed its requirements.
- The size and complexity of the LLP's operations.
- The extent to which the LLP is operating in a high-risk industry.

For some LLPs where they are trading profitably and have adequate working capital the evidence can be fairly minimal.

In other cases, where the position is less certain, it may be necessary to prepare cash flow projections for subsequent periods comparing these with available, or likely to be available, facilities. Where such projections are considered necessary, they should be completed in sufficient detail to take full account of both future trading and the impact of any major transactions—for example proposed acquisitions or major capital investment programmes.

3 FACTORS INDICATING A SIGNIFICANT LEVEL OF CONCERN

12.3 Whether something is significant or not will depend on the circumstances of the individual LLP. There are, however, a number of factors that can be regarded as being indicative of a potential going concern problem. These include:

- An excess of liabilities over assets.
- Net current liabilities.
- Borrowing facilities under negotiation.
- Default on terms of loans and actual or potential breaches of covenants.

- Significant liquidity or cash flow problems.
- Major losses or cash flow problems since the balance sheet date which threaten the LLP's continuing existence.
- Major restructuring of debt.
- Denial of (or reduction in) normal terms of trade by suppliers.
- Fundamental changes in the market or technology to which the LLP cannot adapt adequately.
- Loss of key members or staff.
- Loss of key customers.
- Regulatory changes to which the LLP cannot adapt.
- Major litigation in which an adverse judgment would imperil the LLP's continued existence or seriously damage its reputation.

4 RELIANCE ON THE SUPPORT OF OTHER ENTITIES WITHIN A GROUP

12.4 Where an LLP which is part of a group relies upon its parent or another member of that group for financial support, the auditors will require to see written confirmation that this support will continue to be made available. This is usually done by way of a 'letter of support' issued by the parent to the LLP. The auditors will also need to satisfy themselves that the parent is in a strong enough financial position to provide the necessary support to the LLP.

In some cases a letter of support may be required from the LLP to a subsidiary where that entity's ability to continue as a going concern is dependent upon financial support from the LLP. The LLP should consider the effect such support will have on its own ability to continue in operational existence.

5 ASSESSMENTS MADE BY AUDITORS

12.5 In carrying out their work the auditors will need to assess whether the going concern concept is appropriate and the adequacy of any disclosures made in the accounts.

The auditors will discuss factors affecting the ability of the LLP to continue in business with the members and also examine the financial information available to support the members' opinion, such as the latest management accounts or budgets and forecasts. They may also request copies of other supporting details such as correspondence with bankers and other providers of finance.

The auditors will pay particular attention to the assumptions underlying any cash flow projections, including the following:

- past history as to the reliability of projections prepared by the LLP;
- whether the projected income is reasonable in the context of existing clients and customers and known marketing activity for the future;
- whether assumptions as to profit and levels of work in progress, debtors and creditors are consistent with the history of the business;
- that the assumptions made are consistent with each other;
- that projected and necessary capital expenditure has been included;
- that all payments during the period are taken into account, including members' remuneration and drawings and annuities to former members;
- that those periods where cash is most critical have been identified and that an assessment of headroom above available facilities has been made.

Where critical points within the cash flow are identified, the actions which can be taken by the members to mitigate the impact should be discussed.

6 DISCLOSURE WHERE THERE IS SIGNIFICANT CONCERN

12.6 The adequacy of disclosure made by the members will be assessed by the auditors, but it will not normally be regarded as adequate unless it contains the following:

- A statement that the accounts have been prepared on the going concern basis.
- A statement of the relevant facts.
- A statement of the assumptions made by the members which should be clearly distinguishable from the relevant facts.
- The nature of any material uncertainty.
- Where appropriate and practicable, a statement regarding the members' plans for resolving the matters giving rise to the uncertainty.
- Details of any relevant actions taken by the members.

These statements should be given reasonable prominence within the accounts and are usually best positioned in the accounting policies note under the 'Basis of preparation' heading.

7 REASSESSMENT PRIOR TO SIGNING THE ACCOUNTS

12.7 The members' assessment of going concern and the information supporting that assessment will usually be prepared at a date in advance of the accounts being approved. In addition, the auditors will perform some of their work on the appropriateness of the going concern basis whilst carrying out other fieldwork. This may be completed some time before the accounts are approved. At the time that the accounts are approved the members will need to revisit their assessment and consider any further factors that have come to light up until the date the accounts are approved. The auditors will similarly need to update their procedures by both discussion with the members and by review of any further evidence which has become available.

8 IMPACT ON THE AUDIT REPORT

12.8 There are a number of effects that going concern can have on the audit report dependent on the circumstances of the individual LLP. The auditing standard which provides guidance on going concern assessments (ISA 570) considers all the permutations of circumstances that can arise, the further procedures the auditor may have to undertake and the effect on the audit report. These are summarised in Table 12.1:

Table 12.1 Effects of going concern assessments on audit report

Situation	Impact on audit report
No material uncertainty about ability to continue as a going concern	Unqualified
Material uncertainty about ability to continue as a going concern, but the circumstances are explained fully in the notes to the accounts	Unqualified report but with emphasis of matter paragraph
Material uncertainty about the LLP's ability to continue as a going concern, but the circumstances are not explained fully in the notes to the accounts	Qualified on grounds of disagreement regarding disclosure ('Except for') or adverse opinion

12.8 *Going concern*

Situation	Impact on audit report
The auditors are unable to obtain such information and explanations as they consider necessary from the LLP's management	Qualified on grounds of limitation of scope (Disclaimer)
The period to which the members have paid particular attention in assessing the going concern basis is less than one year from the date of approval of the financial statements, and the auditors believe this to be unreasonably short	Disclaimer as a result of limitation of scope, possibly with disagreement regarding disclosure if the directors have also failed to disclose the period
The period to which the members have paid particular attention in assessing the going concern basis is less than one year from the date of approval of the accounts, but this has been disclosed	Unqualified (including emphasis of matter paragraph where appropriate)
The period to which the members have paid particular attention in assessing the going concern basis is less than one year from the date of approval of the accounts and the members have not disclosed that fact	Qualified on grounds of disagreement regarding disclosure ('Except for')
The auditors disagree with the preparation of the accounts on the going concern basis	Adverse opinion ('Does not give a true and fair view')
The accounts, in order to give a true and fair view, are prepared on a basis other than the going concern basis	Unqualified

Chapter 13

Other accounting standards

1 INTRODUCTION

13.1 There are a number of other accounting standards and UITF abstracts which the preparers and auditors of the accounts of an LLP may need to have particular reference to. These are as follows:

- SSAP 21—'Accounting for leases and hire purchase contracts'
- FRS 15—'Tangible fixed assets'
- FRS 21—'Events after the balance sheet date'
- UITF Abstract 24—'Accounting for start up costs'
- UITF Abstract 29—'Website development costs'
- UITF Abstract 34—'Pre-contract costs'

The main provisions of each of the above as they are likely to affect LLPs are discussed below. However, this chapter does not cover all aspects of the standards that might be relevant to the circumstances of an LLP and reference should be made to the detail of the standard or abstract as considered appropriate.

2 LEASES

13.2 The accounting for leases is covered by SSAP 21 and this identifies three distinct types of arrangement—finance leases, operating leases and hire-purchase contracts.

A Finance leases

13.3 A finance lease is a lease that transfers substantially all the risks and rewards of ownership of an asset to the lessee. Whilst there are a number of factors to consider, SSAP 21 contains the presumption that a transfer of risks and rewards has occurred if at the inception of the lease the present value of the minimum lease payments, including any initial payment, amounts to substantially all (normally 90 per cent or more) of the fair value of the leased asset. In carrying out such a calculation, the present value should be calculated by using the interest rate which is implicit in the lease. Evaluation of leases needs to be carefully considered and a number of leasing companies have 'engineered' their leases so that they fall just outside of the 90 per cent rule and can often therefore be treated as operating leases. The 90 per cent or more presumption can (and should) be rebutted where it clearly does not accord with the commercial reality.

At the inception of a finance lease, both the leased asset and the related lease creditor should be recorded on the balance sheet at the present value of the minimum lease payments. In most cases, the fair value of the asset will be a close approximation. Depreciation should be charged over the shorter of the lease term or the estimated useful life of the asset. The difference between the total minimum lease payments and their present value at the inception of the lease represents a finance charge. This should be allocated to accounting periods over the term of the lease, so as to produce a constant rate of interest (or a reasonable approximation thereof) on the remaining balance of the lease obligation. A 'straight-line' interest charge will rarely achieve the correct result. Each rental payment is apportioned between finance charge and a reduction of the lease creditor. The net book value of assets held under finance leases is required to be disclosed in the accounts along with the depreciation charged thereon.

B Operating leases

13.4 An operating lease is defined as a lease other than a finance lease. Rentals payable under an operating lease should be charged on a straight-line basis over the lease term, even if the payments are not made on that basis.

Property leases give rise to two particular situations where the cash rental payments may be different from the amount that should be charged to the profit and loss account. These are (1) where an LLP has been granted a rent-free period and (2) where it is paying rent on vacant property.

In negotiating a new lease or in renewing an existing lease, the lessor may provide incentives for the LLP to enter into the agreement. Examples of such incentives are an upfront cash payment to the lessee or an initial period of the lease term that may be rent free or at a reduced rent. Such situations are covered by UITF Abstract 28 'Operating lease incentives'. Irrespective of the form the inducement might take, any benefits received and receivable should be treated as a reduction of the total rental expense. The benefit should be spread on a straight-line basis over the shorter of the lease term and the period until the first rent review date on which the rent is adjusted to market rate. As a result there will be a charge to the profit and loss account for rent in a period when no cash payments are being made. For example, an LLP enters into a lease for five years with the first year being rent free and with annual rentals thereafter of £50,000. The charge to the profit and loss account in each of years 1 to 5 will be £40,000.

Provisions for vacant property are dealt with in Chapter 10.

C Hire-purchase contracts

13.5 A hire-purchase contract is a contract for the hire of an asset which includes terms giving the hirer an option to acquire legal title to the asset upon the fulfilment of certain conditions stated in the contract. Hire-purchase contracts should usually be accounted for in the same way as finance leases.

3 TANGIBLE FIXED ASSETS

13.6 FRS 15 deals with accounting for all tangible fixed assets, with the exception of those that are categorised as investment properties, which are subject to the provisions of SSAP 19 'Accounting for investment properties'.

A The 'cost' of a tangible fixed asset

13.7 Tangible fixed assets should first be recorded at cost although, subject to certain conditions, they can be subsequently revalued. Costs which may be capitalised are those that are incremental and would have been avoided only if the asset had not been constructed or acquired. The costs which can be considered for capitalisation are as follows:

- The purchase price, which should be net of any discounts or rebates.
- The labour costs of employees which are directly attributable to construction or acquisition, for example an architectural practice that chooses to design its own property, may include the time of the staff directly involved in the design project.
- Stamp duty, import duties, non-refundable purchase tax; site preparation and clearance costs; initial delivery and handling costs; installation costs; professional fees.

- Where the application of FRS 12 (see Chapter 10) means that a provision is required for the dismantling of an asset and/or restoration of a site at the end of its useful economic life, the estimated cost of dismantling should be included as part of the cost of the asset. For example, if an LLP leases a property and installs partitioning, but the terms of the lease state that this must be removed at the end of the lease, the cost of the partitioning included within fixed assets should also include the estimated cost to dismantle it.

The cost of an asset can include interest on borrowings used to finance the production of that asset, to the extent that those costs arise during the period of production. Capitalisation of finance costs is an optional policy, but if the LLP chooses to capitalise finance costs it must do so for all fixed assets where finance costs are a material element of the cost. The interest that may be capitalised should relate only to borrowings that would have been avoided if there had been no expenditure on the asset. This does not mean, however, that there needs to be a separately identifiable loan. The funds could arise from using existing cash which could otherwise have been used to repay existing borrowing or from the extended use of existing facilities.

B Maintenance expenditure versus enhancement

13.8 Subsequent expenditure, which is necessary to ensure that the fixed asset can continue to operate at the same level, should be charged to the profit and loss account as it is incurred. Subsequent expenditure should only be capitalised where it enhances the performance of the fixed asset in excess of its previous capabilities, for example by increasing its life or capacity. If a fixed asset comprises distinct, different components and these are depreciated at different rates, expenditure to restore 'worn out' parts of the asset can be capitalised.

C Revaluation

13.9 Tangible fixed assets may be revalued, but where an LLP adopts a policy of revaluation all assets within the same class must be revalued. The classes of fixed asset defined by the LLPA are very broad, namely land and buildings; plant and machinery; and fixtures, fittings, tools and equipment. An LLP could adopt a narrower class so long as this is reasonable. It is rare that assets other than property are subject to revaluation.

The decision to revalue a class of assets is one which should only be entered into after careful consideration as there can be significant costs associated with complying with the requirements contained in the accounting standard. FRS 15 requires that there must be a full, detailed valuation at least once every five years which must be carried out by a qualified valuer. Where the valuer is internal to the LLP, the valuation is required to be reviewed by an external independent valuer. In addition an interim valuation by a qualified internal or external valuer is required in year 3 and reviews should also be performed in years 1, 2 and 4 if there are indications of a material change in value. Valuations are required to be carried out in accordance with the RICS guidance for the appropriate type of property.

D Depreciation

13.10 The general principle is that tangible fixed assets should be depreciated to their recoverable amount over their useful expected life. Prior to the issue of FRS 15 a number of companies put forward arguments as to why fixed assets, particularly property, should not be depreciated. These were typically based on the charge being immaterial, because the asset had a very long life and/or the residual value was very high and close to the carrying value, as a result of high levels of maintenance expenditure. Whilst FRS 15 acknowledges that depreciation might be immaterial, it requires reporting entities to go through a process of proving it. Where no depreciation is charged or an asset is estimated to have a useful life in excess of 50 years, an annual impairment review is required. In determining whether or not depreciation is immaterial, reference should be had not only to its effect on the financial period under review, but also to the effect on the accounts of cumulative levels of non-depreciation.

4 ACCOUNTING FOR EVENTS AFTER THE BALANCE SHEET DATE

13.11 The LLPA requires that all liabilities and losses which have arisen or are likely to arise relating to the period prior to the balance sheet date should be taken into account. This includes those which only become apparent between the balance sheet date and the date on which the accounts are approved by the members. Such items are referred to as 'events after the balance sheet date', the accounting for which is dealt with by FRS 21.

FRS 21 distinguishes between two types of event:

- adjusting events, which are those that result in an adjustment of the accounts; and

- non-adjusting events, which are those that may require disclosure but which do not require adjustment to amounts included in the accounts.

A Adjusting events

13.12 Adjusting events are those occurring after the balance sheet date which provide additional evidence of conditions that were in existence at that date. The accounts should be changed to take account of this additional evidence. Examples of adjusting events include:

- The subsequent determination of the purchase price or of the proceeds of sale of assets purchased or sold before the year end.
- A valuation of a property that provides evidence of an impairment in value.
- The receipt of a copy of the financial statements or other information in respect of an unlisted company in which the LLP has an interest that provides evidence of an impairment in the value of a long-term investment.
- The receipt of proceeds of sales after the balance sheet date or other evidence concerning the net realisable value of stocks.
- The receipt of evidence that the previous estimate of accrued profit on a long-term contract was materially inaccurate.
- The renegotiation of amounts owing by debtors or the insolvency of a debtor.
- The discovery of errors or frauds which show that the financial statements were incorrect.

Events after the balance sheet date which indicate a deterioration in operating results and in the financial position of the LLP may highlight issues as to whether the accounts should be prepared on a going concern basis (see Chapter 12).

B Non-adjusting events

13.13 Non-adjusting events relate to conditions which did not exist at the balance sheet date. They do not result in the accounts requiring amendment, but should be disclosed if they are so material that non-disclosure would affect the ability of users of the accounts to have a proper understanding of the financial position of the LLP. FRS 21 includes the following examples of non-adjusting events:

- A major business combination after the balance sheet date or disposal of a major subsidiary.
- Announcing a plan to discontinue an operation.
- Major purchases and disposals of assets, or expropriation of major assets by government.
- The destruction of a major production plant by a fire after the balance sheet date.
- Announcing or commencing the implementation of a major restructuring.
- Abnormally large changes after the balance sheet date in asset prices or foreign exchange rates.
- Entering into significant commitments or contingent liabilities, for example, by issuing significant guarantees.
- Commencing major litigation arising solely out of events that occurred after the balance sheet date.

Whilst these are listed as non-adjusting events, the circumstances surrounding them should always be considered. In some cases, it may be that they are the best indicator of circumstances at the balance sheet date where no other evidence is available.

5 START-UP COSTS

13.14 UITF Abstract 24 only permits the costs incurred at the start up phase of a business to be treated as an asset where they meet the requirements of another accounting standard, for example FRS 15. 'Start-up costs' are defined widely and include costs arising from one-time activities related to opening a new facility, introducing a new product or service, conducting business in a new territory, conducting business with a new class of customer, initiating a new process in an existing facility, starting a new operation and any similar items. Start-up costs also include the costs of relocating or reorganising part or all of an entity (these may, however, meet the criteria set out in FRS 12—see **10.6**), costs related to organising a new entity, and expenses and losses incurred both before and after opening.

Whilst at first sight UITF Abstract 24 may appear to be at odds with the accruals basis of accounting, the UITF was looking to the Statement of Principles' definition of an asset and determined that such costs did not meet that definition. Accordingly, start-up costs should be expensed as they are incurred in the same way as similar costs incurred in the remainder of the business.

6 WEBSITE DEVELOPMENT COSTS

13.15 The growth in the use of the Internet and doubts over how entities should account for the often significant levels of cost associated with the development of websites led to the issue of UITF Abstract 29 which deals specifically with website development costs.

The costs of building a website can typically be analysed into four parts.

- *Planning costs.* These will include, for example, the costs of undertaking feasibility studies, determining the objectives and functionalities of the website, researching the ways of achieving the required functionalities, identifying appropriate hardware and web applications and selecting suppliers and consultants. Planning costs are unlikely to give rise to future economic benefits for the LLP and therefore should not be capitalised but be charged to the profit and loss account as they arise.
- *Application and infrastructure development costs.* These include the costs of obtaining and registering a domain name and of buying or developing hardware and operating software that relate to the functionality of the site.
- *Design costs.* Expenditure to develop the design and appearance of individual website pages.
- *Content costs.* Expenditure incurred on preparing, accumulating and posting the website content.

Application and infrastructure development costs, design costs and content costs may give rise to an asset. Design and content costs should only be capitalised if the website is capable of generating revenues directly, for example by enabling orders to be placed. In order to meet the criteria for recognition as an asset the following criteria must be met:

- the expenditure must be separately identifiable;
- the technical feasibility and commercial viability of the website should have been assessed with reasonable certainty in the light of factors such as likely market conditions (including competing products), public opinion and possible legislation;
- the website should be capable of generating sales or other revenues directly (see below) and the expenditure incurred should be making a contribution to the ability of the website to generate income;
- there is a reasonable expectation that the present value of the future cash flows (ie future revenues less attributable costs) to be generated by the website will be no less than the amounts capitalised; and

- adequate resources exist, or are reasonably expected to be available, to enable the website project to be completed and to meet any consequential need for increased working capital.

One of the key criteria in determining whether or not the costs may be capitalised is the ability of the website to generate income and this income must be capable of being measured separately. A large number of websites are in effect just another method of advertising and it will not be possible to separate income generated from the website from that generated from other sources. In these circumstances the costs should be written off to the profit and loss account as they are incurred.

Website costs should be treated as a tangible fixed asset and maintenance expenditure should be charged to the profit and loss account as incurred. The website development costs should be depreciated over their estimated useful economic life and given the rapid rate of technological innovation, the useful economic life of a website is likely to be short. The risk of impairment is also significantly higher than with many other tangible fixed assets. Where the design or content of a website requires more frequent replacement than the website as a whole, it may be appropriate to select a depreciation period for the cost of the design or content that is shorter than the depreciation period selected for the remainder of the asset.

7 PRE-CONTRACT COSTS

13.16 When it was issued, UITF Abstract 34 was aimed at providing guidance to those entities that incur substantial costs in bidding for contracts, particularly in respect of PFI and PPP contracts. However, the accounting principles are equally applicable to all entities including those LLPs who as part of their business are regularly involved in tendering for contracts.

The costs of tendering can be significant and a number of different accounting treatments have emerged ranging from capitalising all costs into the cost of the contract, to writing everything off to the profit and loss account. UITF Abstract 34 provides codification of the correct treatment.

In general pre-contract costs should be expensed as they are incurred. The only exception to this is that costs which are directly attributable to obtaining a contract may be capitalised once it is 'virtually certain' that the contract will be won and it is clear that the cash flows from the contract will be sufficient to recover those costs.

The exact time at which a contract will become virtually certain will depend upon the contract. One criterion, however, is that there should only be one bidder remaining in the tendering process, although this fact alone is not sufficient to assume that the contract is virtually certain. The award of the contract should also be expected within a reasonable timescale and the contractual arrangements should be sufficiently detailed to allow the assessment of future cash flows to be made. If the award is subject to a future event (for example, regulatory approval) it cannot be regarded as virtually certain.

It is only those costs incurred from the point at which the contract becomes virtually certain that may be capitalised, it is not possible to capitalise costs incurred before that date retrospectively.

Chapter 14

The transition from partnership to LLP

1 INTRODUCTION

14.1 The combination of the advantages of limited liability and the concept of partnership makes conversion of existing partnerships to LLP status attractive. It is not however without its costs, not only in respect of the internal time and professional fees involved in making the transfer, but also with regard to the accounting and auditing requirements, a number of which will be unfamiliar to a number of partnerships that choose to 'convert' (see below). In addition, the financial affairs of the LLP will be in the public domain through the filing of annual accounts with the Registrar of Companies.

In this chapter we look specifically at some of the accounting issues surrounding the transition of a partnership to an LLP.

2 HOW MUCH CAPITAL?

14.2 Whereas the liability of individual members is significantly reduced from that within a partnership, in the event of the insolvency of the LLP the capital may not be returned to the members. It is important, therefore, to take this into consideration when determining the level of existing partnership capital which should be introduced to the new LLP. Although there are obvious attractions to keeping the level of capital as low as possible, it should be noted that third parties such as banks may require the subordination of amounts due to members and/or require minimum amounts to be retained within the LLP.

3 THE ASSETS AND LIABILITIES TO BE TRANSFERRED

14.3 In most circumstances it would be anticipated that all, or the vast majority of, assets and liabilities would be transferred from the partnership to the new LLP. The former partners may, however, decide that some assets and liabilities should remain in the former partnership.

One particular area for consideration is the treatment of liabilities to former partners. Some partnerships have sought to leave the retirement benefits due to former partners as a liability of the partnership rather than transfer that liability to the LLP. Such a course of action will normally require the consent of those former partners and they may also require the liabilities to be underwritten by the LLP. The accounting treatment of post-retirement liabilities is dealt with in Chapter 6. Similar accounting treatment will also apply to any other liabilities of the former partnership—namely whether or not the LLP will be required to recognise the liability will depend upon the probability that it may be required to make any payment. Even if no provision is required to be recognised in the accounts, the possibility of a future liability should be disclosed as a contingent liability of the LLP.

4 ALIGNMENT OF ACCOUNTING POLICIES

14.4 On transferring assets and liabilities to the LLP, the amounts at which they are initially recorded in the accounts should be calculated by reference to the accounting policies to be adopted by the LLP. Dependent on the policies adopted by the partnership, these could vary significantly from those shown in the accounts of the predecessor partnership. This will be particularly relevant where the partnership had prepared accounts for its own purposes other than on the 'true and fair' basis, making adjustments to that basis only for the purposes of its tax return. Areas where differences may arise include:

- Provisions for retirement benefits to former partners to the extent that the liability to meet the cost is transferred to the LLP (see Chapter 6).
- De-recognition of provisions which do not meet the definition within FRS 12 (for example, provisions for possible future PI claims) (see Chapter 10).

The particular problems facing those partnerships with subsidiary undertakings are discussed below.

5 GROUPS

14.5 The majority of partnerships with subsidiary undertakings, irrespective of whether those subsidiaries are companies or other partnerships, will not historically have prepared consolidated accounts in the form required by accounting standards. The partnership may well have prepared some form of 'group' accounts, probably an aggregation of the results and balance sheets, however these are unlikely to be sufficient going forward.

There are a number of steps that the LLP must take in order to establish the basis on which any group accounts should be constructed. It will need to:

- Ascertain those investments of the partnership which fall to be treated as subsidiaries. In simple terms this will be those other entities in which the LLP has a controlling interest. (see Chapter 2.)
- Determine whether or not group accounts are required by reference to the combined size of the LLP and its subsidiaries. (See Chapter 2.)
- Determine the cost of investment in those subsidiaries. For companies, this will be the amount paid to acquire the shares, which should already be recorded as an investment in the accounts of the partnership. For an investment in a partnership, the cost of investment will be the amount of capital held in that partnership.
- Where a subsidiary has been previously acquired, ascertain whether or not it is practical to determine the fair values of assets and liabilities at the date of acquisition.
- Where a subsidiary is a company or partnership formed by the previous partnership to undertake certain parts of the partnership's business (typically in a different geographical region) no further analysis should be necessary.
- If intra-group trading is significant, identify the amounts as these will need to be eliminated from consolidated accounts.
- Where assets are sold between group members at a profit (for example, fixed assets or stock), the profit element will need to be identified in order that it can be eliminated from the consolidated accounts.

Of the above, the step which is most likely to cause difficulties is the identification of assets and liabilities associated with past acquisitions. Whether or not it is possible to determine the fair value of assets and liabilities at the date of acquisition will depend on the extent of the records maintained by the partnership and the period of time that has elapsed since the acquisition. The method suggested below will usually give an adequate approximation, particularly for subsidiaries acquired some time previously.

14.6 As a matter of accounting principle the consolidated accounts should not include any profits earned by a subsidiary prior to acquisition. An adjustment should therefore be made in the consolidated accounts to remove any such profits from the cumulative reserves of the group. The 'other side' to this adjustment should be made against the cost of investment, along with the elimination of the share capital of the subsidiary. Any difference between the cost of investment and pre-acquisition reserves and share capital, together with any adjustments to reflect fair value should be treated as goodwill and be amortised in the consolidated profit and loss account.

The following example illustrates the position where it has not been possible to determine the fair values of the assets and liabilities in a previously acquired subsidiary.

Example

X & Co (a partnership) acquired Y Ltd a number of years ago for £200. At that date profit and loss reserves were £70. At the current year end the balance sheet of Y Ltd is as follows:

	£
Assets	400
Share capital	30
Profit and loss account	370
	400

In preparing the consolidated accounts, the newly formed LLP will raise a journal which will debit share capital by £30, debit profit and loss by £70, debit goodwill by £100 (£200 - £100) and credit cost of investment by £200. The goodwill will then require amortisation in accordance with the accounting policy determined by the LLP.

---

6 PRESENTING THE TRANSITION IN THE ACCOUNTS

14.7 As discussed in Chapter 9, the transition from partnership to LLP should be accounted for using the merger basis so long as it meets the criteria to be treated as a group reconstruction set out in FRS 6 'Acquisitions and mergers'. FRS 6 is worded in the context of corporate entities and states that in order to qualify as a group reconstruction 'the ultimate shareholders must remain the same, and the rights of each such shareholder, relative to the others, should be unchanged' immediately before and after the transaction.

Putting this definition into the context of a partnership, in order for the transfer to an LLP to qualify as a group reconstruction and hence for merger accounting, the interests of members in the LLP should be in the same proportions as their 'share' in the partnership immediately prior to transfer. Both the amount of capital introduced and profit sharing arrangements will need to be taken into account when determining if the criteria have been met.

The application of this requirement means that transition to an LLP should not be combined with the retirement or appointment of partners or members, nor should the relative benefits of partners/members be altered at this stage. Such changes may also have consequences in respect of the exemption from stamp duty on incorporation. However, HMRC have stated that it will accept that there can be a change of partners taking place the instant before or after incorporation. The Stamp Office is likely to ask to see all associated documents affecting the change in membership prior to and/or after incorporation.

Where the requirements of FRS 6 are not met, the transfer should be accounted for as an acquisition and the assets and liabilities transferred would need to be restated to their fair values and the 'consideration' for the acquisition determined by reference to the value of the business of the partnership transferred. Goodwill will arise as a consequence of the difference between the two values and this will have to be recognised on the balance sheet and amortised through the profit and loss account of the LLP. For a partnership in the services sector, the value of the business taken as a whole compared to the value of its underlying assets and liabilities could well be significantly different. The amount of goodwill, and the impact on the profit and loss account, could be substantial.

14.8 The SORP requires that single entity LLPs formed from the transfer or incorporation of an existing entity should present comparative pro forma information for the previous period. The corresponding amounts should be stated using the same accounting policies as those adopted by the LLP. For the reasons discussed above, the amounts shown by the comparative figures may differ from those in the equivalent partnership accounts resulting in a consequent difference between partners' interests and members' interests. This difference should not be reflected in the accounts of the LLP which should be prepared on the basis that the LLP has always existed and always prepared accounts in accordance with its selected accounting policies.

It is frequently the case that there is a delay between forming the LLP and the transfer of the existing partnership undertaking. In these cases there is a conflict between the requirements to present a profit and loss account that complies with statutory requirements (ie covering only the period from the transfer of the previous undertaking) and information that provides a meaningful comparative of what is effectively the same business. The SORP considers this issue in some detail in Appendix 3 and recommends the following presentation:

- A statutory profit and loss account for the period from transfer of business to the reporting date.
- Disclosure of the 12-month period to the reporting date.
- Pro forma comparatives for the previous reporting period.

Where a group transfers to LLP status, FRS 6 requires that comparative figures be presented for the previous year. These will not be pro forma and will, therefore, fall within the scope of the audit report. Whilst an LLP presenting consolidated accounts does not have to present the individual LLP's profit and loss account within the financial statements, CA 85 requires that it still be prepared for the information of members. Similar principles to those discussed above will therefore apply.

It is recommended that those partnerships considering transfer to LLP status carry out some initial calculations of the impact changes in accounting policies could have and how this affects existing partners' interests. Such changes can then be explained and discussed with the partners.

7 AUDIT ISSUES ARISING IN THE FIRST YEAR OF TRANSITION

14.9 There are a number of potential issues which will affect the audit of an LLP formed from a partnership in its first year.

The majority of partnerships do not have their accounts audited and therefore it will be for the auditors to determine whether they are able to obtain sufficient evidence as to the accuracy of the opening balance sheet of the LLP to enable them to state that the accounts for the current reporting period give a true and fair view. Whilst it should usually be possible to form an opinion on the closing balance sheet, the opening figures will impact the amounts included in the profit and loss account and qualification with respect to limitation in audit scope may be required.

It may be possible to restrict the qualification to a specific account area, for example work in progress, if the auditors are able to perform audit procedures that allow them to meet the requirements of ISA 510 'Initial engagements – opening balances and continuing engagements – opening balances'.

Further complications may arise in considering the status of any comparative figures and their impact on the audit report.

For a single entity LLP formed from an existing partnership the comparative information is only included as a pro forma and can therefore be excluded from the scope of the audit report. Where this is the case, the presentation of the comparatives in the accounts should make it clear that they are unaudited pro forma information and this fact should also be made clear in the scope paragraph of the audit report.

The position for a group headed by a new LLP which is required to present comparative information in accordance with FRS 6 may be more complex. In particular, where the comparative information has not been subject to audit, reference to this fact will be required in the audit report in a similar way to that referred to above.

Appendix 1

LLP proforma accounts

XYZ LLP

REPORT AND ACCOUNTS

FOR THE YEAR ENDED

31 MARCH 200X

NOTE – in this example all profits are divided after the year end and capital is returned to members on their retirement.

Contents

Designated members and advisers

Designated members
A Designate
B Smith
C Jones

Registered office
1 The Long Street
Longtown
Longshire
LL1 1XY

Bankers
Big Bank plc
85 The Long Street
Longtown
Longshire
LL1 1YZ

Auditors
Stuart & Wilson LLP
5 The Short Street
Longtown
Longshire
LL2 1AB

Solicitors
Wright & Prentice LLP
25 The Short Street
Longtown
Longshire
LL2 1BC

Registered number
OC3 54321

Members' report

The members present their report and the accounts for the year ended 31 March 200X.

Activities

The principal activity of the LLP continues to be [ ]. The subsidiary, ABC Limited's, principal business is [ ].

Review of business

In the opinion of the members the state of the company's affairs at 31 March 200X is satisfactory.

During the year the LLP acquired the entire share capital of ABC Limited. Further details can be found in note 2.

Designated members

The following were designated members during the year:

A Designate

B Smith

C Jones

Members' drawings and the subscription and repayment of members' capital

During the year members receive monthly drawings representing payments on account of profits which may be allocated to them. The amount of such drawings is set at the beginning of each financial year, taking into account the anticipated cash needs of the LLP and may be reclaimed from members until such time as profits have been allocated to them.

Profits are determined, allocated and divided between members after the finalisation of the accounts. Prior to the allocation of profits and their division between members, drawings are included within debtors. Unallocated profits are included within 'members' other interests'.

Capital requirements are determined by the designated members and are reviewed at least annually. All members are required to subscribe a proportion of that capital, with the amounts being determined by reference to experience.

On retirement, capital is repaid to members.

Donations

During the year the group made donations for charitable purposes of £[ ].

Auditors

A resolution to reappoint Stuart & Wilson LLP as auditors will be proposed at the next members' meeting.

Approved by the members

and signed on their behalf

A Designate

Designated member

Statement of members' responsibilities in respect of the accounts[1]

Legislation applicable to limited liability partnerships requires the members to prepare accounts for each financial year which give a true and fair view of the state of affairs of the [LLP/group] and of the profit or loss of the [LLP/group] for that period. In preparing those accounts, the members are required to:

- select suitable accounting policies and then apply them consistently;
- make judgements and estimates that are reasonable and prudent;
- state whether applicable accounting standards have been followed, subject to any material departure disclosed and explained in the accounts[2];
- prepare the accounts on the going concern basis unless it is inappropriate to presume that the LLP will continue in business.

The members are responsible for keeping proper accounting records which disclose with reasonable accuracy at any time the financial position of the LLP and to enable them to ensure that the accounts comply with the Limited Liability Partnerships Regulations. They are also responsible for safeguarding the assets of the [LLP/group] and thence for taking reasonable steps for the prevention and detection of fraud and other irregularities.

These responsibilities are exercised by the designated members on behalf of the members.

1 This statement can alternatively be included within the members' report and is only required where the LLP is subject to audit.
2 Required only for LLPs that do not meet the definition of small or medium-sized.

Independent auditors' report to the members of XYZ LLP

We have audited the group and parent LLP accounts ('the accounts') of XYZ LLP for the year ended 31 March 200X which comprise the consolidated profit and loss account, the consolidated and LLP balance sheets, the consolidated cash flow statement, the consolidated statement of total recognised gains and losses, the consolidated note of historical cost profits and losses and the related notes 1 to 24. These accounts have been prepared under the accounting policies set out therein.

This report is made solely to the members, as a body, in accordance with Section 235 of the Companies Act 1985, as applicable to limited liability partnerships. Our audit work has been undertaken so that we might state to the members those matters we are required to state to them in an auditors' report and for no other purpose. To the fullest extent permitted by law, we do not accept or assume responsibility to anyone other than the LLP and the LLP's members as a body, for our audit work, for this report, or for the opinions we have formed.

Respective responsibilities of members and auditors

As described in the Statement of Members' Responsibilities, the members are responsible for the preparation of the accounts in accordance with applicable law and United Kingdom Accounting Standards (United Kingdom Generally Accepted Accounting Practice).

Our responsibility is to audit the accounts in accordance with relevant legal and regulatory requirements and International Standards on Auditing (UK and Ireland).

We report to you our opinion as to whether the accounts give a true and fair view and are properly prepared in accordance with the Companies Act 1985 as applicable to limited liability partnerships. We also report to you if, in our opinion, the Members' Report is not consistent with the accounts, if the LLP has not kept proper accounting records and if we have not received all the information and explanations we require for our audit.

We read the Members' Report and consider the implications for our report if we become aware of any apparent misstatements within it.

Basis of audit opinion

We conducted our audit in accordance with International Standards on Auditing (UK and Ireland) issued by the Auditing Practices Board. An audit includes examination, on a test basis, of evidence relevant to the amounts and disclosures in the accounts. It also includes an assessment of the significant estimates and judgements made by the members in the preparation of the accounts, and of whether the accounting policies are appropriate to the LLP's circumstances, consistently applied and adequately disclosed.

We planned and performed our audit so as to obtain all the information and explanations which we considered necessary in order to provide us with sufficient evidence to give reasonable assurance that the accounts are free from material misstatement, whether caused by fraud or other irregularity or error. In forming our opinion we also evaluated the overall adequacy of the presentation of information in the accounts.

Opinion

In our opinion:

- the accounts give a true and fair view, in accordance with United Kingdom Generally Accepted Accounting Practice, of the state of the group's and parent LLP affairs as at 31 March 200X and of the group's profit [loss] for the year then ended; and
- the accounts have been properly prepared in accordance with the Companies Act 1985 as applicable to limited liability partnerships.

Stuart & Wilson LLP
Chartered Accountants
Registered Auditors

5 The Short Street
Longtown
Longshire, LL2 1AB

Date

Consolidated profit and loss account for the year ended 31 March 200X

	Notes	200X		200Y
		£'000	£'000	£'000
Turnover	3			
– Acquisitions				
Operating costs				
Staff costs	5			
Depreciation and other amounts written off tangible fixed assets				
Other operating charges				
Other operating income				
Operating profit				
– Acquisitions				
Profit/(loss) on sale of fixed asset investments				
Interest receivable and similar income				
Interest payable and similar charges	6			
Profit on ordinary activities before taxation[3]	7			
Tax on profit on ordinary activities[3]	8			

3 Applicable only where the LLP has subsidiaries that are tax paying.

	Notes	200X £'000	200X £'000	200Y £'000
Profit for the financial year before members' remuneration and profit shares				
Members' remuneration charged as an expense	4			
Profit for the financial year available for division among members[4]	4			

All of the LLP's operations are classed as continuing. [There were no gains or losses in either year other than those included in the above profit and loss account][5].

4 In circumstances where all profits are automatically divided before the year end this amount will be zero.

5 Disclosure required where there are no recognised gains and losses other than the profit or loss for the year and no STRGL is presented.

Consolidated statement of total recognised gains and losses for the year ended 31 March 200X

	200X £'000	200Y £'000
Profit for the financial year available for division among members		
Unrealised surplus on revaluation of properties		
Total recognised gains and losses for the year		

Consolidated note of historical cost gains and losses

Profit for the financial year available for division among members		
Difference between the historical cost depreciation charge and the actual depreciation charge for the year calculated on the revalued amount		
Historical cost profit for the financial year		

Consolidated balance sheet as at 31 March 200X

	Notes	**200X £'000**	**200Y £'000**
Fixed assets			
Intangible assets	10		
Tangible assets	11		
Investments	12		
Current assets			
Work in progress	13		
Debtors	14		
Cash at bank and in hand			
Creditors: amounts falling due within one year	15		
Net current assets/(liabilities)			
Total assets less current liabilities			
Creditors: amounts falling due after more than one year	16		
Provisions for liabilities	18		
Net assets attributable to members before pension fund surplus/(deficit)[6]			
[Pension fund surplus/(deficit)] [6]			
NET ASSETS ATTRIBUTABLE TO MEMBERS			

6 Position of net pension fund surplus/(deficit) where the LLP has a defined benefit pension scheme.

	Notes	200X £'000	200Y £'000
REPRESENTED BY			
Loans and other debts due to members within one year			
Members' capital classified as a liability under FRS 25[7]	19		
Other amounts	19		
Equity			
Members' other interests – other reserves classified as equity under FRS 25[8]	19		
Revaluation reserve	19		
Total members' interests			
Amounts due from members			
Loans and other debts due to members			
Members' other interests			

The accounts were approved by the members on [ ] and were signed on its behalf by:

A Designate

Designated member

7 In this example members' capital is returned on retirement and is therefore a liability.
8 Profits which are only divided after the year end would be included within this balance.

Balance sheet as at 31 March 200X

	Notes	**200X £'000**	**200Y £'000**
Fixed assets			
Intangible assets	10		
Tangible assets	11		
Investments	12		
Current assets			
Work in progress	13		
Debtors	14		
Cash at bank and in hand			
Creditors: amounts falling due within one year	15		
Net current assets/(liabilities)			
Total assets less current liabilities			
Creditors: amounts falling due after more than one year	16		
Provisions for liabilities	18		
Net assets attributable to members before pension fund surplus/(deficit) [6]			
Pension fund surplus/(defict)[6]			
NET ASSETS ATTRIBUTABLE TO MEMBERS			

	Notes	**200X** **£'000**	**200Y** **£'000**
REPRESENTED BY			
Loans and other debts due to members within one year			
Members' capital classified as a liability under FRS 25[7]			
Other amounts			
Equity			
Members' other interests – other reserves classified as equity under FRS 25[8]			
Revaluation reserve			
Total members' interests			
Amounts due from members			
Loans and other debts due to members			
Members' other interests			

The accounts were approved by the members on [ ] and were signed on its behalf by:

A Designate

Designated member

Consolidated cash flow statement for the year ended 31 March 200X

	Notes	**200X** **£'000**	**200Y** **£'000**
Net cash inflow/(outflow) from operating activities	a		
Returns on investments and servicing of finance			
Interest received			
Interest paid			
Interest element of finance lease rental payments			
Net cash inflow/(outflow) from returns on investments and servicing of finance			
Taxation			
Corporation tax paid			
Capital expenditure and financial investment			
Payments to acquire tangible fixed assets			
Receipts from sales of tangible fixed assets			
Purchase of fixed asset investments			
Purchase of trademarks			
Net cash inflow/(outflow) for capital expenditure and financial investment			
Acquisitions and disposals			
Purchase of subsidiary undertaking			
Net cash/(overdraft) acquired with subsidiary			

	Notes	**200X £'000**	**200Y £'000**
Net cash inflow/(outflow) from acquisitions and disposals			
Transactions with members and former members			
Drawings and distributions to members			
Capital contributions by members			
Capital repayments to members			
Net cash inflow/(outflow) from transactions with members and former members			
Cash inflow before management of financing			
Financing			
New long-term loans			
Repayment of long-term loans			
Repayment of capital element of finance lease rentals			
Net cash inflow/(outflow) from financing			
Increase/(decrease) in cash in the year	b		

Notes to the cash flow statement

	200X	200Y
a **Reconciliation of operating profit/(loss) to net cash inflow/(outflow) from operating activities**	**£'000**	**£'000**
Operating profit/(loss)		
Depreciation		
Amortisation of intangible assets		
Loss/(profit) on sale of tangible fixed assets		
Decrease/(increase) in work in progress		
Decrease/(increase) in debtors		
Increase/(decrease) in creditors		
Net cash inflow/(outflow) from operating activities		
b **Reconciliation of net cash flow to movement in net debt**		
Increase/(decrease) in cash in the year		
Cash inflow/(outflow) from increase/(decrease) in debt		
Change in net debt resulting from cash flows		
Other non-cash items:		
New finance leases		
Movement in net debt in the year		
Net debt at 1 April 200Y		
Net debt at 31 March 200X		

Notes to the cash flow statement *(continued)*

c **Analysis of net debt**	**At 1 April 200Y**	**Cash flow**	**Other non-cash changes**	**At 31 March 200X**
	£'000	**£'000**	**£'000**	**£'000**
Cash in hand, at bank				
Overdrafts				
Debt due after 1 year				
Debt due within 1 year				
Finance leases				
Total				

Notes to the accounts for the year ended 31 March 200X

1 Accounting policies[9]

The accounts have been prepared in accordance with applicable accounting standards and the requirements of the Statement of Recommended Practice 'Accounting by limited liability partnerships'. A summary of the significant accounting policies adopted are described below.

Basis of accounting

The accounts have been prepared under the historical cost convention, modified by the revaluation of certain tangible fixed assets and investments.

Basis of consolidation

The accounts consolidate the results and the assets and liabilities of the LLP and its subsidiary.

Acquisitions

On the acquisition of a business, fair values are attributed to the groups' share of net separable assets. Where the cost of acquisition exceeds the fair values attributable to such net assets, the difference is treated as purchased goodwill and capitalised in the balance sheet in the year of acquisition. The results and cash flows relating to an acquired business are included in the consolidated cash flow statement from the date of acquisition.

Goodwill and other intangible assets

Goodwill arising on acquisition is the difference between the fair value of the consideration given and the fair value of the net assets acquired. It is included on the balance sheet and is being amortised over a period of ten years. Trademarks are included at cost of acquisition and are depreciated over their estimated useful life of three years.

Fixed assets

Depreciation is provided on cost or revalued amounts in equal annual instalments over the estimated useful lives of the assets concerned. The following annual rates are used.

9 The accounting policies shown here are illustrative and the policies disclosed should be those that are specific to the LLP.

Fixtures and fittings –	15% reducing balance
Office equipment –	20% reducing balance
Motor vehicles –	25% reducing balance

Investments

Investments are included at cost less any provision for impairment

Investments in subsidiaries are included at cost less any provision for impairment.

Deferred taxation

Deferred tax is provided for on a full provision basis on all timing differences which have arisen but not reversed at the balance sheet date. *[No timing differences are recognised in respect of (i) property revaluation surpluses where there is no commitment to sell the asset; (ii) gains on sale of assets where those gains have been rolled over into replacement assets; and (iii) additional tax which would arise if profits of overseas subsidiaries are distributed except where otherwise required by accounting standards].* A deferred tax asset is not recognised to the extent that the transfer of economic benefit in the future is uncertain. Any assets and liabilities recognised have not been discounted.

Members' remuneration[10]

Profits attributable to members are determined, allocated and divided between members after the year and until that time are included within members' other interests. Any drawings paid in respect of those profits are included within debtors.

The terms of the members' agreement require that capital be returned to a member on his or her retirement. They are accordingly accounted for as liabilities of the LLP.

Retirement benefits

Contributions to defined contribution schemes are charged to the profit and loss account as they become payable in accordance with the rules of the scheme.

Under the terms of the membership agreement former members are entitled to payment based on a formula directly linked to the profits of the LLP. Provision is made in the accounts for the estimated present value of the expected future payments to that member. Amounts in respect of

10 The accounting policy reflects the particular profit sharing and capital arrangements of the LLP in this example.

current members are included within members' remuneration charged as an expense, and amounts with respect to former members are included within staff costs. The liability with respect to current members is included within loans and other amounts due to members and the liability to former members is included within provisions for liabilities. The unwinding of the discount of the provision for retirement benefits is charged to the profit and loss account and included in interest payable.

The liability is reassessed annually and any changes in the estimates are included within the profit and loss account.

Leases

Assets held under finance leases are included in fixed assets and the capital element of the related lease commitment is shown as obligations under finance leases. The lease rentals are treated as consisting of capital and interest elements. The capital element is applied to reduce the outstanding obligations and the interest element is charged against profit over the period of the lease.

Rental costs under operating leases are charged to the profit and loss account on a straight-line basis over the lease term.

Foreign currencies

Transactions denominated in a foreign currency are translated into sterling at the rate of exchange ruling at the date of the transaction. At the balance sheet date, monetary assets and liabilities denominated in foreign currency are translated at the rate ruling at that date. All exchange differences are dealt with in the profit and loss account.

Work in progress

Work in progress comprises direct staff costs and a share of overhead appropriate to the relevant state of completion of the related project. The relevant proportion of the salaried remuneration of members is included within work in progress. Members' profit allocations are excluded. The overhead attributable to all time incurred by members and included within work in progress is included within the valuation.

Revenue recognition

Revenue in respect of professional services is recognised by reference to the fair value of the services provided at the balance sheet date as a proportion of the total value of the engagement. Unbilled revenue is included within debtors as accrued income.

2 **Acquisition**

During the year the LLP acquired the entire share capital of ABC Limited for cash consideration of £[ ]. In addition, the former shareholders of ABC Limited have been offered an enhanced allocation of profits in addition to that available to all members, which is calculated by reference to a formula linked to the financial performance of ABC Limited. An amount of £[ ], being the current best estimate of the amounts payable, is included in members' other interests. The acquisition has been accounted for using the acquisition method of accounting. The amount of goodwill arising as a result of the acquisition is £[ ]. This is included on the group balance sheet.

The profits after taxation of ABC Limited were as follows:

	Profit after tax £'000
Results prior to acquisition	
1 April 200Y to date of acquisition	
Preceding financial year ended 31 March 200Y	

The following table summarises the adjustments made to the book value of the major categories of assets and liabilities acquired to arrive at the fair values included in the consolidated accounts at the date of acquisition.

	Book amount £'000	**Fair value adjust-ments £'000**	**Fair value £'000**
Tangible fixed assets			
Current assets			
Creditors			
Consideration			
Cash (including acquisition costs of £[ ])			
Contingent consideration			
Goodwill			

The fair value adjustments comprise [ ]

The profit and loss account includes the following amounts attributable to the acquired business: turnover £[ ], cost of sales £[ ], gross profit £[ ], administrative expenses £[ ] and operating profit £[ ].

3 **Turnover**[11]

	200X	**200Y**
	£'000	**£'000**
United Kingdom		
Other European countries		

4 **Information in relation to members**

	200X	**200Y**
	Number	**Number**
The average number of members during the year was		
	£'000	*£'000*
[*The average members' remuneration during the year was*[12]		]
	£'000	£'000
Salaried remuneration of members		
Paid under employment contract		
Paid under the terms of the LLP agreement		

11 Analysis only required where there is more than one class of business or geographic segment.

12 This disclosure is optional.

	200X Number	**200Y Number**
The amount of profit attributable to the member with the largest entitlement was		

Profit attributable to the member with the largest entitlement is determined by reference to [ ]

5 **Employee information**

The average number of persons (including members with contracts of employment) employed by the LLP during the year was:

	200X Number	**200Y Number**
Selling and distribution		
Administration		

	£'000	**£'000**
Staff costs for the above persons were:		
Wages and salaries		
Social security costs		
Pension costs		

6 **Interest payable and similar charges**

	200X £'000	**200Y £'000**
Bank loans and overdrafts		
On finance leases		
Unwinding of discount in relation to retirement benefits		

7 Profit on ordinary activities before taxation

	200X £'000	200Y £'000
Profit on ordinary activities before taxation is stated after charging/(crediting):		
Depreciation		
– owned assets		
– assets held under finance leases		
Goodwill amortisation		
Amortisation of intangible assets		
Hire of plant and machinery – operating leases		

The analysis of auditors' remuneration is as follows:

	200X £'000	200Y £'000
Fees payable to the LLP's auditors for the audit of the LLP's annual accounts		
Fees payable to the LLP's auditors and their associates for other services to the group		
The audit of the LLP's subsidiaries pursuant to legislation		
Total audit fees		
Tax services		
Corporate finance services		
Other services		
Total non-audit fees		

	200X	**200Y**
	£'000	**£'000**
Fess payable to the LLP's auditors in respect of associated pension schemes		
Audit		

8[3] **Tax on profit on ordinary activities**

	£	**£**
UK corporation tax at [ ]%		
Under/(over) provision in respect of prior years		
Deferred tax		

The standard rate of tax for the year, based on the UK standard rate of corporation tax is [ ]%. The actual tax charge for the current and previous year is less than the standard rate for the reasons set out in the following reconciliation.

	200X	**200Y**
	£	**£**
Profit on ordinary activities before tax		
Tax on profit on ordinary activities at standard rate		
Factors affecting charge for the period:		
Profits of LLP not chargeable to corporation tax		
Capital allowances for period in excess of depreciation		
Expenses not allowable for tax purposes		
Other timing differences		

	200X	**200Y**
	£	**£**
Profit on sale of fixed asset covered by rollover relief		
Adjustments to tax charge in respect of prior periods		

9 **Profit of the LLP**

As permitted by section 230 of the Companies Act (as modified for application to LLPs), the LLP is exempt from presenting its own profit and loss account. The profit of the LLP for the financial year amounted to £[ ] (200Y: £[ ]).

10 **Intangible fixed assets**

Group

	Goodwill	**Trademarks**	**Total**
	£'000	**£'000**	**£'000**
Cost			
At 1 April 200Y			
Additions			
At 31 March 200X			
Amortisation			
At 1 April 200Y			
Charge for year			
At 31 March 200X			

Group

	Goodwill £'000	Trademarks £'000	Total £'000
Net book value			
At 31 March 200X			
At 31 March 200Y			

LLP

	Trademarks £'000
Cost	
At 1 April 200Y	
Additions	
At 31 March 200X	
Amortisation	
At 1 April 200Y	
Charge for the year	
At 31 March 200X	
Net book value	
At 31 March 200X	
At 31 March 200Y	

11 **Tangible fixed assets**

Group	**Freehold land and buildings**	**Office fixture and fittings**	**Motor vehicles**	**Total**
	£'000	**£'000**	**£'000**	**£'000**
Cost or valuation				
At 1 April 200Y				
Additions				
Acquired with subsidiary				
Disposals				
Adjustment arising on revaluation				
At 31 March 200X				
Depreciation				
At 1 April 200Y				
Charge for the year				
Disposals				
Adjustment arising on revaluation				
At 31 March 200X				
Net book value				
At 31 March 200X				
At 31 March 200Y				

Comparable amounts determined according to the historical cost convention.

Group	**Freehold land and buildings**	**Office fixture and fittings**	**Motor vehicles**	**Total**
	£'000	**£'000**	**£'000**	**£'000**
Cost				
Accumulated depreciation				
Net book value				
At 31 March 200X				
At 31 March 200Y				

The net book value of the group's office fixtures and fittings includes £[ ] (200Y: £[ ]) in respect of assets held under finance leases.

LLP	**Freehold land and buildings**	**Office fixtures and fittings**	**Motor vehicles**	**Total**
	£'000	**£'000**	**£'000**	**£'000**
Cost or valuation				
At 1 April 200Y				
Additions				
Disposals				
Adjustments arising on revaluation				
At 31 March 200Y				

LLP	Freehold land and buildings	Office fixtures and fittings	Motor vehicles	Total
	£'000	£'000	£'000	£'000
Depreciation				
At 1 April 200Y Charge for the year Disposals Adjustments arising on revaluation				
At 31 March 200Y				
Net book value				
At 31 March 200Y				
At 31 March 200Y				

Comparable amounts determined according to the historical cost convention.

Cost				
Accumulated depreciation				
Net book value				
At 31 March 200X				
At 31 March 200Y				

Freehold land and buildings are held at a valuation. All such assets were subject to a full valuation at 31 March 200X, by Mssrs House & Co, Chartered Surveyors.

12 Investments

Group

	Shares £'000
At 1 April 200Y	
Additions	
Disposals	
At 31 March 200X	

LLP

	Shares £	**Investment in subsidiary undertaking £**	**Total £**
At 1 April 200Y			
Additions			
Disposals			
At 31 March 200X			

The LLP has the following investments in subsidiary undertakings:

	Country of registration	**Activity**	**Portion of ordinary shares held**
ABC Limited	[ ]	[ ]	[ ]

13 **Work in progress**

	Group		LLP	
	200X	**200Y**	**200X**	**200Y**
	£'000	**£'000**	**£'000**	**£'000**
Work in progress				

14 **Debtors**

	Group		LLP	
	200X	**200Y**	**200X**	**200Y**
	£'000	**£'000**	**£'000**	**£'000**
Trade debtors				
Amounts owed by subsidiary undertaking				
Amounts due from members				
Other debtors				
Prepayments and accrued income				

15 **Creditors:** amounts falling due within one year

	Group		LLP	
	200X	**200Y**	**200X**	**200Y**
	£'000	**£'000**	**£'000**	**£'000**
Bank loans and overdrafts				
Obligations under finance leases				
Trade creditors				
Amounts owed to subsidiary undertaking				
Corporation tax				
Other taxation and social security				
[Retirement benefits due to former members][13]				
Other creditors				
Accruals and deferred income				

16 **Creditors:** amounts falling due after more than one year

	Group		LLP	
	200X	**200Y**	**200X**	**200Y**
	£	**£**	**£**	**£**
Bank loans and overdrafts				
Obligations under finance leases				
[Retirement benefits due to former members][13]				

13 Where the amount of retirement benefits to former members is fixed it should be included within creditors rather than provisions (split between due within and due after one year).

17 Borrowings

	Group		LLP	
	200X	**200Y**	**200X**	**200Y**
	£	**£**	**£**	**£**
Bank overdraft				
Bank loan (secured [ ]% above LIBOR)				
Obligations under finance leases				
Due within one year				
Due after one year				
Maturity analysis				
Within one year or on demand				
More than one year but less than two years				
More than two years but not less than five years				
More than five years				

18 **Provisions for liabilities**

Group and LLP

	Post-retirement payments to former members £'000	**Provisions for dilapidations £'000**	**Total £'000**
At 1 April 200Y			
Subsidiary acquired			
Profit and loss account charge			
Amortisation of discount			
At 31 March 200X			

19 Reconciliation of members' interests – Group

	Members' equity interests				Loans and other debts due to members			
	Members' capital classed as equity	Revaluation reserve	Other reserves	Total	Members' capital classed as a liability	Other amounts	Total	Total
	£'000	£'000	£'000	£'000	£'000	£'000	£'000	£'000
Amounts due to members								
Amounts due from members								
Members' interests at [ ]								
Members' remuneration charged as an expense								
Profit for the financial year available for discretionary division among members								
Members' interests after profit for the year								
Other divisions of profits/losses								
Surplus arising on revaluation of fixed assets								
Introduced by members								
Repayments of capital								

	Members' equity interests				Loans and other debts due to members			
	Members' capital classed as equity	**Revaluation reserve**	**Other reserves**	**Total**	**Members' capital classed as a liability**	**Other amounts**	**Total**	**Total**
	£'000	**£'000**	**£'000**	**£'000**	**£'000**	**£'000**	**£'000**	**£'000**
Repayment of debt								
Drawings								
Other movements								
Amounts due to members								
Amounts due from members								
Members' interests at [ ]								

19 Reconciliation of members' interests – LLP

	Members' equity interests				Loans and other debts due to members			
	Members' capital classed as equity	Revaluation reserve	Other reserves	Total	Members' capital classed as a liability	Other amounts	Total	Total
	£'000	£'000	£'000	£'000	£'000	£'000	£'000	£'000
Amounts due to members								
Amounts due from members								
Members' interests at [ ]								
Members' remuneration charged as an expense								
Profit for the financial year available for discretionary division among members								
Members' interests after profit for the year								
Other divisions of profits/losses								
Surplus arising on revaluation of fixed assets								
Introduced by members								
Repayments of capital								

	Members' equity interests				Loans and other debts due to members			
	Members' capital classed as equity	Revaluation reserve	Other reserves	Total	Members' capital classed as a liability	Other amounts	Total	Total
	£'000	£'000	£'000	£'000	£'000	£'000	£'000	£'000
Repayment of debt								
Drawings								
Other movements								
Amounts due to members								
Amounts due from members								
Members' interests at [ ]								

20 ***Pension costs***

The group operates a defined benefit scheme in the UK. A full actuarial valuation was carried out at 31 March 200Y and updated to 31 March 200X by a qualified independent actuary. The major assumptions used by the actuary were:

	At 31/03/0X	***At 31/03/0Y***
Rate of increase in salaries		
Rate of increase in pensions in payment		
Discount rate		
Inflation assumption		

The assets in the scheme and the expected rate of return were:

	Long-term rate of return expected at 31/03/0X £'000	***Value at 31/03/0X £'000***	***Long-term rate of return expected at 31/03/0Y £'000***	***Value at 31/03/0Y £'000***
Equities				
Bonds				
Property				
Total market value of assets				
Present value of scheme liabilities				
Surplus/(deficit) in scheme				

LLP proforma accounts

	200X	*200Y*	*200Z*
	£'000	*£'000*	*£'000*
Analysis of amount charged to operating profit			
Current service cost			
Past service cost			
Analysis of amount debited to net interest receivable/payable			
Expected return on pension scheme assets			
Interest on pension scheme liabilities			
Net charge for year			

Analysis of amount recognised in the statement of total recognised gains and losses

	200X	*200Y*	***200Z***
	£'000	*£'000*	***£'000***
Excess of actual return over expected return on pension scheme assets			
Experience (gains)/losses on pension scheme liabilities			
Changes in assumptions underlying the present value of the pension scheme liabilities			
Actuarial gain/(loss) recognised in STRGL			

LLP proforma accounts

	200X	*200Y*	***200Z***
	£'000	*£'000*	***£'000***
History of experience gains and losses			
Difference between the expected and actual return on pension scheme assets			
Amount			
Percentage			
Experience gains and losses on pension scheme liabilities			
Amount			
Percentage			
Total recognised in the STRGL			
Amount			
Percentage			

Movement in surplus/(deficit) during the year

	200X	***200Y***
	£	***£***
Surplus/(deficit) in scheme at beginning of the year		
Movement in year:		
Current service cost		
Contributions		
Past service costs		
Other finance income		
Actuarial gain		
Surplus/(deficit) in scheme at end of year		

The full actuarial valuation at 31 December 200Y showed an increase in the surplus from [ ] to [ ]. Improvements in benefits costing [ ] were made in 200X and contributions reduced to [ ] ([ ] of pensionable pay). It has been agreed with the trustees that contributions for the next three years will remain at that level.

21 **Operating lease commitments**

At 31 March 200X the LLP had annual commitments under operating leases for fixtures and fittings as follows:

	200X Other £'000	200Y Other £'000
For leases expiring:		
Within one year		
Between two and five years		

22 **Capital commitments**

	200X £	200Y £
Contracted but not provided for		

23 **Contingent liabilities**

The LLP has guaranteed the borrowings of individual members taken out in order to fund their capital interests in the LLP. At 31 March 200X the total amount guaranteed was £[ ]. 200Y £[ ].

24 **Controlling party**

In the opinion of the members there is no controlling party as defined by Financial Reporting Standard No 8 'Related party disclosures'.

Appendix 2

LLP disclosure checklist

Note: this disclosure checklist does not consider the circumstances where an LLP may be able to adopt the Financial Reporting Standard for Smaller Entities (FRSSE)

1 GENERAL

		Reference	*Yes/no/na*
True and fair view			
1.1	The accounts must show a true and fair view, having regard to the substance of any arrangement or transaction. Where necessary the additional information needed to achieve this should be disclosed.	s 226(4)	
1.2	Where, in special circumstances, compliance with the Act, accounting standards or the SORP would result in the accounts not giving a true and fair view, departure from the provision may be made to the extent necessary for the accounts to give a true and fair view. The following must be disclosed: • A clear statement that there has been a departure and that this is necessary in order for the accounts to give a true and fair view. • Explanation of the treatment normally required and that actually adopted.	s 226(5), FRS 18.62	

		Reference	*Yes/no/na*
	• Explanation of why the prescribed treatment would not give a true and fair view. • Description of how the position in the accounts differs as a result of the treatment adopted, together with quantification unless this is already evident from the accounts or it cannot be readily quantified, in which case the circumstances should be explained.		
Reporting the substance of transactions			
1.3	Whether or not a single transaction or arrangement, or a group or series of transactions, results in assets or liabilities being recognised or ceasing to be recognised, disclosure should be sufficient to enable the commercial effect to be understood.	FRS 5.30	
1.4	Where a transaction has resulted in the recognition of assets or liabilities whose nature differs from that of items usually included under the relevant balance sheet heading, the differences should be explained.	FRS 5.31	
1.5	Where, following a legal transfer of an asset, there is no significant change in the right to benefits, or exposure to risk, the legal transfer should be disclosed.	FRS 5.67	
1.6	Where, in exceptional cases, there is a significant change in the rights to benefits and exposure to risks, but an asset continues to be recognised, the description or amount relating to the asset should, where necessary, be changed and a liability recognised for any obligations to transfer benefits that are assumed. This will occur in the following circumstances: • a transfer of only part of the item in question;	FRS 5.23	

		Reference	*Yes/no/na*
	• a transfer of all of the item for only part of its life; and • a transfer of all of the item for all of its life but where the entity retains some significant right to benefits or exposure to risk.		
	Where there is uncertainty over gains or losses and they could have an effect on the profit and loss account, this fact should be disclosed in the accounts.	FRS 5.24	
1.7	Where FRS 5 requires a linked presentation for certain non-recourse finance arrangements, disclose the following:		
	• The related finance as a deduction from the gross asset on the face of the balance sheet within a single asset category.	FRS 5.26	
	• State explicitly that the LLP is not obliged to support any losses, nor does it intend to do so.	FRS 5.27	
	• Confirm that the provider of the finance has agreed in writing that the principal and interest will only be repaid to the extent that sufficient funds are generated by the specific item to be financed, and that it will not seek recourse in any other form.	FRS 5.27	
	• Show the net income or expense in the profit and loss account, and the gross components by way of note.	FRS 5.28	

2 FORMATS

		Reference	*Yes/no/na*
2.1	Items included in the formats may be shown in greater detail.	Sch 4.3(1)	
2.2	Additional items may be added to the formats.	Sch 4.3(2)	

		Reference	*Yes/no/na*
2.3	Disclose the particulars of, and reasons for, a change in the format of either the balance sheet or the profit and loss statement.	Sch 4.3(2)	
2.4	Where items which are assigned arabic numerals in the formats have been combined in the accounts, include the individual amounts in the notes.	Sch 4.3(4)	
2.5	Omit headings or subheadings which have nil amounts for both the current and previous year.	Sch 4.3(5), Sch 4.4(3)	
2.6	Assets may not be offset against liabilities. Income may not be offset against expenses.	Sch 4.5, Sch 4.14	

3 CORRESPONDING AMOUNTS

		Reference	*Yes/no/na*
3.1	In respect of every item in the primary statements and notes to the financial statements the corresponding amount for the immediately preceding accounting period should be shown.	FRS 28.6, FRS 28.10(a)	
3.2	Where there is no amount to be included in the primary statements or notes to the financial statements for the current period but a corresponding amount can be shown, this amount should be shown.	FRS 28.8	
3.3	Where a corresponding amount is not comparable to the current period it must be adjusted and the particulars of and reasons for the adjustment must be disclosed in the notes to the accounts.	FRS 28.9, FRS 28.10(b)	
3.4	Corresponding amounts are not required to be disclosed with respect to the following:	FRS 28.11	

		Reference	*Yes/no/na*
	• Details of additions, disposals, revaluations, transfers and cumulative depreciation of fixed assets. • Transfers to or from members' interests. • Accounting treatment of acquisitions. • Details of shareholdings in subsidiary undertakings. • Significant holdings in undertakings other than subsidiary undertakings.		

4 MEMBERS' REPORT

		Reference	*Yes/no/na*
4.1	State the principle activities of the LLP (and its subsidiary undertakings) during the period together with any significant changes.	SORP 29 s 234(2)	
4.2	A fair review of the development of the business of the LLP and its subsidiaries during the period and their position at the period end.	s 234(1)(a), s 246(4)(a)	
4.3	Particulars of any important post-balance sheet events affecting the LLP (and subsidiary undertakings).	Sch 7.6(a)	
4.4	An indication of the likely future developments in the business of the LLP (and subsidiary undertakings).	Sch 7.6(b)	
4.5	Give an indication of any research and development activities of the LLP (and subsidiary undertakings).	Sch 7.6(c)	
4.6	Give an indication of the existence of branches of the LLP outside the UK.	SORP 29 Sch 7.6(d)	
4.7	Any significant difference between the book value and market value of interests in land and buildings held by the LLP (and subsidiary undertakings).	Sch 7.1(2)	

		Reference	*Yes/no/na*
4.8	The identity of anyone who was a designated member during the year.	SORP 29	
4.9	The policy under which members contribute or subscribe amounts to the LLP by way of equity or debt.	SORP 62	
4.10	Policy regarding members' drawings and the subscription and repayment of members' capital subscribed or otherwise contributed by members. This should include details of the policy applicable where the cash requirements of the business compete with the need to allow cash drawings by the members.	SORP 29, 62	
4.11	Any transfers of members' interests from equity to debt (and vice versa) during the period and up to the date the accounts are approved.	SORP 62	
4.12	Where the LLP has made any donation to any registered party or to any other EU political organisation, or incurred any EU political expenditure, and the amount of the donation or expenditure, or the aggregate amount of all donations and expenditure, exceeded £200 disclose: • The name of each registered party or other EU organisation to whom any donation has been made. • The total amount given to that party or organisation by way of such donations in the period. • The total amount of EU political expenditure incurred within the period.	PPERA 2000, s 140.3(2)	

		Reference	*Yes/no/na*
4.13	Where any of the LLP's subsidiaries have made any donation to any registered party or to any other EU political organisation, or incurred any EU political expenditure, and the total amount of any such donations or expenditure made by the LLP and the subsidiaries between them exceeded £200 disclose: • The name of each registered party or other EU organisation to whom any donation has been made. • The total amount given to that party or organisation by way of such donations in the period. • The total amount of EU political expenditure incurred within the period.	PPERA 2000, s 140.3(3)	
4.14	Where the LLP has made any contribution to a non-EU political party, and it does not have any subsidiaries which have made such contributions, disclose: • A statement of the amount of the contribution; or • Where the LLP has made two or more such contributions in the period, a statement of the total amount of the contributions.	PPERA 2000, s 140.4(1)	
4.15	Where any of the LLP's subsidiaries have made any contribution to a non-EU political party, disclose the total amount of the contributions made in the period by the LLP and the subsidiaries between them.	PPERA 2000, s 140.4(2)	
4.16	Where the LLP has given money exceeding £200 for charitable purposes and it does not have any subsidiaries which have given any money for such purposes, disclose, for each of the purposes for which money was given, the amount given for that purpose.	PPERA 2000, s 140.5(1)	

		Reference	*Yes/no/na*
4.17	Where any of the LLP's subsidiaries have given money for charitable purposes and the amount given in that period for such purposes by the company and the subsidiaries between them exceeds £200, disclose for each of the purposes for which money has been given by the LLP and the subsidiaries between them, a statement of the amount of money given for that purpose.	PPERA 2000, s 140.5(2)	

4.18	If at any time during the period the LLP failed to qualify as small or medium and was part of a group of which the parent was a public limited company, then in respect of the period immediately following that covered by the accounts disclose:
	• Whether in respect of some or all of its suppliers it is the LLP's policy to follow any code or standard on payment practice and, if so, the name of the code or standard, and the place where information about, and copies of, the code or standard can be obtained.
	• Whether in respect of some or all of its suppliers it is the LLP's policy:
	  • to settle the terms of payment with those suppliers when agreeing the terms of each transaction;
	  • to ensure that those suppliers are made aware of the terms of payment; and
	  • to abide by the terms of payment.
	• Where the policy differs from either of the above include an explanation of what the policy is.
		Sch 7.12	

		Reference	*Yes/no/na*
	• Where the policy is different for different suppliers or classes of suppliers, the identity of those suppliers or classes of suppliers. • In respect of the financial period covered by the report, the number of creditor days, calculated by dividing the period end trade creditors by the total amount invoiced by suppliers during the period, multiplied by the number of days in the period.		

5 STATEMENT OF MEMBERS' RESPONSIBILITIES

		Reference	*Yes/no/na*
5.1	The statement of members' responsibilities is only required where the accounts require an audit. It may be included within the members' report or be presented as a separate statement (usually immediately before the audit report).	APB Bulletin 2006/06	
5.2	The statement should contain an adequate description of members' responsibilities including the following: • The requirements of legislation for members to prepare true and fair accounts. • The members are required to select suitable accounting policies, apply them on a consistent basis and make judgements and estimates that are prudent and reasonable. • For large LLPs only, the members are required to state whether suitable accounting standards have been followed subject to material departures which are disclosed and explained in the accounts.	APB Bulletin 2001/1	

		Reference	*Yes/no/na*
	• The members are required to prepare the accounts on a going concern basis unless it is not appropriate to presume that the LLP will continue in business. • The members' responsibility for keeping proper accounting records, safeguarding the assets and taking reasonable steps for the prevention and detection of fraud and other irregularities. • Where the financial statements are to be published on the LLP's web-site, a statement that the members are responsible for the maintenance and integrity of the website and that legislation in the UK governing the preparation and dissemination of financial statements may differ from other jurisdictions.		

6 AUDITORS' REPORT

		Reference	*Yes/no/na*

6.1	The audit report should include the following:
	• The term 'Independent Auditor' in the title.
	• An introductory paragraph which clearly identifies the accounts subject to audit.
	• Description of the respective responsibilities of members and auditors including:
	  • members' responsibilities or a cross-reference to the separate statement;
	  • clear identification of the national financial reporting and auditing framework;
		APB Bulletin 2006/06	

		Reference	*Yes/no/na*
	• auditors' responsibilities; • auditor's responsibilities to read the members' report and any other information presented with the accounts for apparent misstatements and inconsistencies with the accounts; • the auditor's opinion on the accounts; • the manuscript or printed signature of the auditors; and • the date of the auditors' report.		
6.2	The following should be disclosed in relation to the auditors: • The firm's name. • Qualification (eg registered auditors). • Address.	APB Bulletin 2006/06	
6.3	The auditors are required to state in their report if in their opinion: • Proper accounting records have not been kept, or proper returns from branches not visited by the auditors have not been received, or the accounts are not in accordance with the accounting records or returns. • All the information and explanations necessary for the purposes of their audit have not been obtained.	s 237	
6.4	Where there are material undisclosed related party transactions or an undisclosed control relationship that are required to be disclosed under FRS 8, the relevant information should be included in the opinion section of the audit report whenever practicable.	ISA 550. 116-2	

		Reference	*Yes/no/na*
6.5	The audit report must refer to any significant departure from SSAPs/FRSs/SORP: • Which is not adequately disclosed in the notes to the accounts. • With which the auditors do not concur.		

7 PROFIT AND LOSS ACCOUNT

		Reference	*Yes/no/na*
Format			
7.1	The following items must be shown on the face of the profit and loss account:		
	• Turnover (in group accounts this should include share of any joint venture turnover, but not as part of group turnover).	FRS 9.21	
	• Operating profit (in group accounts, share of associate operating result should be shown immediately after group operating result and share of joint venture operating result (if any). Any amortisation or write-down of goodwill arising on acquiring the associate or joint venture should be charged at this point and disclosed.)	FRS 9.21	
	• Exceptional profits or losses on the sale or termination of an operation.	FRS 3.20	
	• Exceptional costs of a fundamental reorganisation or restructuring having a material effect on the nature and focus of the LLP's operations.	FRS 3.20	
	• Exceptional profits or losses on the disposal of fixed assets.	FRS 3.20	

		Reference	*Yes/no/na*
	• The above should be analysed, on the face of the profit and loss account between continuing, discontinued and acquired operations.	FRS 3.14	
	• Profit or loss on ordinary activities before taxation.	Sch 4 F	
	• For group accounts, at or below the level of profit before tax, include the LLP's share of the relevant amount for joint ventures and associates within the amounts for the group, and for items below this level disclose the amounts relating to joint ventures.	FRS 9.21, 27	
	The following may be shown either on the face of the profit and loss account or in the notes:		
	• Other operating income.	Sch 4 F	
	• Income from shares in group undertakings.	Sch 4A 21	
	• Income from participating interests (in consolidated accounts, this is replaced by two items: 'Income from interests in associated undertakings' and 'Income from other participating interests').	Sch 4 F	
	• Income from other fixed asset investments.	Sch 4 F	
	• Other interest receivable and similar income.	Sch 4 F	
	• Amounts written off investments.	Sch 4 F	
	• Interest payable and similar charges.	Sch 4 F	
	(For group accounts disclose the group's share of any FRS 3(20) exceptional items or interest relating to joint ventures or associates separately.)		

		Reference	Yes/no/na
	• Other finance costs – this will include unwinding of discounts on provisions and the net interest cost and return on assets in relation to accounting for defined benefit pension schemes under FRS 17.	FRS 12.48 FRS 17.56	
	• Tax on profit or loss for the financial year.	Sch 4 F	
	• Profit or loss on ordinary activities after taxation.	Sch 4 F	
	• Minority interests.	Sch 4 F	
	• Profit or loss for the financial year before members' remuneration and profit shares.	SORP 44, Sch 4	
	• Members' remuneration charged as an expense.	SORP 44	
	• Profit or loss for the financial year available for discretionary division among members.	SORP 44	
Formats 1 and 3			
7.2	Disclose either on the face of the profit and loss account or in the notes the following:		
	• Cost of sales.	Sch 4 F	
	• Gross profit or loss (format 1 only).	Sch 4 F	
	• Distribution costs.	Sch 4 F	
	• Administrative expenses.	Sch 4 F	
Formats 2 and 4			
7.3	Disclose either on the face of the profit and loss account or in the notes the following:		
	• Change in stocks of finished goods and work in progress.	Sch 4 F	
	• Own work capitalised.	Sch 4 F	
	• Raw materials and consumables.	Sch 4 F	
	• Other external charges.	Sch 4 F	

		Reference	*Yes/no/na*
	• Staff costs: • wages and salaries; • social security costs; • other pension costs.	Sch 4 F	
	• Depreciation and other amounts written off tangible and intangible fixed assets.	Sch 4 F	
	• Exceptional amounts written off current assets.	Sch 4 F	
	• Other operating charges.	Sch 4 F	
Discontinued and acquired operations			
7.4	Where there are no acquisitions or discontinued operations during the current or preceding year, state this immediately below the profit and loss account. Where there have been discontinued or acquired operations complete the remainder of this section.	FRS 3.14	
7.5	Turnover and operating profit must be analysed on the face of the profit and loss account between continuing, acquired and discontinued businesses.	FRS 3.14	
7.6	There must be an analysis (either on the face of the profit and loss account or in the notes to the accounts) of all other statutory headings between turnover and operating profit between continuing, acquired and discontinued businesses.	FRS 3.14	
7.7	Where interest and tax are allocated between continuing and discontinued businesses disclose the assumptions used in making the allocations.	FRS 3.14	
7.8	Where an acquisition or a sale or termination has had a material impact on a major business segment disclose this fact.	FRS 3.15, FRS 6.28	

		Reference	*Yes/no/na*
7.9	For each material acquisition and for other acquisitions in aggregate, the post-acquisition results to the end of the current period should be disclosed in the accounts. Where it is not practicable to determine these amounts, an indication of the contribution of the acquisition to turnover and operating profit should be included. If an indication of the contribution of an acquisition to the results of the period cannot be given, this fact and the reason should be explained.	FRS 3.16, FRS 6.29	
7.10	In the notes to the profit and loss account disclose any costs, following the acquisition, incurred in reorganising, restructuring or integrating the acquisition.	FRS 6.31	
7.11	For discontinued operations, disclose the write-down of assets and any provisions made in earlier periods, analysed between the operating loss and the loss on sale or termination of the discontinued operation, on the face of the profit and loss account immediately below the relevant item.	FRS 3.18, FRS 10.54	
Depreciation and impairment			
7.12	Total charge for depreciation or provision in respect of impairment and, where appropriate, the amount of any provision for impairment written back.	Sch 4.19 FRS 15.100(c)	
7.13	For each class of tangible fixed assets where there has been a change in the following during the period and the effect is material, disclose the financial effect: • Estimate of useful economic lives. • Estimate of residual values.	 FRS 15.100(d) FRS 15.100(d)	

		Reference	*Yes/no/na*
	• Change in depreciation method used. Disclose the reason for any change in depreciation method.	FRS 15.102 FRS 15.102	
7.14	The non-depreciation of investment properties represents a departure from the requirements of the Act. Reference to this departure should be disclosed in the accounts.	SSAP 19.10	
Particulars of members			
7.15	Average number of members in the period	SORP 63 Sch 4.56A(1)	
7.16	Explain the nature of any salaried remuneration of members and analyse it between amounts paid under employment contracts and other amounts.	SORP 24	
7.17	Where the amount of the profit of the LLP before member's remuneration and profit share exceeds £200,000, disclose the amount of profit (including remuneration) attributable to the member with the largest entitlement to profit. The LLP should disclose the policy applied to determine the amount of profit attributable to the member with the largest entitlement to profit and this policy should be applied consistently. Where the LLP has an unconditional right to avoid paying an amount of remuneration or profit, the policy for determining the disclosable amount should be disclosed and should explain how current year unallocated profits and current year allocations of both current and prior year profits are treated.	SORP 64 Sch 4.56A(3) SORP 65	

		Reference	*Yes/no/na*
7.18	If the LLP discloses average members' remuneration, this should be calculated by dividing 'profit before members' remuneration and profit shares' by the average number of members. Where other figures are disclosed these should be reconciled to those calculated by reference to the above method.	SORP 66	
Employees			
7.19	Total average monthly employees by category.	Sch 4.56(1)	
7.20	Disclose separately the aggregate amounts for the period of: • Wages and salaries. • Social security costs. • Other pension costs.	Sch 4.56(4)	
Other profit and loss items			
7.21	Interest payable and similar charges should be disclosed across the following categories: • Loans from group undertakings. • Bank loans and overdrafts. • On other loans.	 Format note 4.16 Sch 4.53(2)(a) Sch 4.53(2)(b)	
7.22	Gains or losses on the repurchase or early settlement of own debt should be disclosed as a separate item within or adjacent to 'interest payable and similar charges'.	FRS 4.64	
7.23	Finance charges on finance leases and hire purchase contracts	s 246(2), SSAP 21.53	
7.24	Amortisation of intangible assets.		
7.25	Amount charged to the profit and loss account for the hire of plant and machinery.	SSAP 21.55	

		Reference	*Yes/no/na*
7.26	Lessees should recognise the benefit of any incentive on a new or renewed operating lease as a reduction of the rental payable, allocated over the shorter of the lease term and a period ending on a date from which it is expected that the prevailing market rental will be payable.	UITF 28.14	

7.27	• Fees payable to the LLP's auditors for the audit of the LLP's annual accounts.
	• Fees payable to the LLP's auditors and their associates for other services to the group.
	• Fees payable to the LLP's auditors in respect of the audit of the LLP's subsidiaries pursuant to legislation.
	• Fess payable to the auditors for other services across the following headings:
	  • Tax services.
	  • Information technology services.
	  • Internal audit services.
	  • Valuation and actuarial services.
	  • Litigation services.
	  • Recruitment and remuneration services.
	  • Corporate finance services.
	  • Other services.
	• Fees payable to the LLP's auditors and their associates in respect of associated pension schemes.
	  • Audit.
	  • Specify any other fees.
		SI 2005/2417	

		Reference	*Yes/no/na*
7.28	Where the LLP is a holding company with a plc subsidiary, or part of a banking or insurance group, or exceeds the criteria multiplied by 10 for defining a medium-sized LLP, disclose the total amount of research and development charged in the profit and loss account analysed between current period's expenditure and amounts amortised from deferred expenditure.	SSAP 13.22, 31	
7.29	The net amount of exchange gains and losses on foreign currency borrowings (less deposits).	SSAP 20.60(a)	
7.30	Amounts written off in respect of research and development.		
Exceptional items			
7.31	The amount and description of each exceptional item, either individually or as an aggregate of similar items, should be disclosed by way of note, or on the face of the profit and loss account if that degree of prominence is necessary to give a true and fair view, together with a statement of the effect of the item.	Sch 4.57(3) FRS 3.19	
7.32	The following should be shown separately on the face of the profit and loss account, after operating profit but before interest: • Profits or losses on the sale or termination of an operation. • Costs of a fundamental reorganisation or reconstruction having a material effect on the LLP's operations. • Profits or losses on the disposal of fixed assets.	FRS 3.20	
7.33	Exceptional items should, where appropriate, be attributed to continuing or discontinued operations.	FRS 3.19	

		Reference	*Yes/no/na*
7.34	The incidence of extraordinary items is expected to be rare. Where they do arise the amounts and description should be disclosed.	FRS 3.22	
Taxation (groups with corporate subsidiaries only)			
7.35	The following elements of the current tax expense or income for the period should be shown separately: • UK tax. • Foreign tax. The amounts should be analysed to separately identify: • Current period. • Adjustments recognised in respect of prior periods.	FRS 16.17	
7.36	Deferred tax should be recognised in the profit and loss account unless it relates to an item included in the statement of total recognised gains and losses.	FRS 19.34	
7.37	The notes to the accounts should show the amount of deferred tax charged or credited to the profit and loss account analysed across the following headings: • The origination and reversal of timing differences. • Changes in tax rates and laws. • Adjustments to the estimated recoverable amounts of deferred tax assets. • Where deferred tax is discounted – changes in the amounts of discount.		
7.38	Circumstances that affect the current and total tax charges or credits for the current period or may affect the current and total charges or credits in future periods, including:	FRS 19.64	

		Reference	*Yes/no/na*

	• A reconciliation of the current tax charge or credit on ordinary activities for the period to the current tax charge that would result from applying a relevant standard rate of tax to the profit on ordinary activities.
	• Basis on which the standard rate of tax has been determined.
	• Where deferred tax has not been recognised on asset revaluation gains or losses, or market values of assets are disclosed:
	  • an estimate of the tax payable or recoverable if the assets were sold at the values shown;
	  • the circumstances in which tax would be payable or recoverable; and
	  • an indication of the amount that may become payable or recoverable in the foreseeable future.
	• Where the entity has sold an asset but not recognised deferred tax on the gain because it will be rolled over:
	  • the conditions that will have to be met to obtain rollover relief; and
	  • an estimate of the tax that would become payable if those conditions were not met.
	• Where a deferred tax asset has not been recognised on the grounds of insufficient evidence of recoverability:
	  • the amount not recognised; and
	  • the circumstances in which it would be recovered.		

		Reference	*Yes/no/na*
Joint ventures			
7.39	If consolidated accounts are not prepared then, unless the LLP is exempt from preparing consolidated accounts, or would be if it had subsidiaries, show the following information by producing a separate set of financial statements or by showing the relevant amounts, together with the effects of including them, as additional information to the LLP's own financial statements: • Share of joint venture turnover but not as part of group turnover. • Share of joint venture operating result, immediately after group operating result; any amortisation or write-down of goodwill arising on acquiring the joint venture should be charged at this point and disclosed. • Share of any FRS 3.20 exceptional items or of interest separately from amounts relating to the group. • At or below the level of profit before tax, include the LLP's share of the relevant amount for joint ventures within the amounts for the group and for items below this level disclose the amounts relating to joint ventures.	FRS 9.21	
Associates			
7.40	If consolidated accounts are not prepared then, unless the LLP is exempt from preparing consolidated accounts or would be if it had subsidiaries, show the following information by producing a separate set of financial statements or by showing the relevant amounts, together with the effects of including them, as additional information to the company's own financial statements:	FRS 9.48	

		Reference	Yes/no/na
	• Associate turnover must be clearly distinguished from group turnover if a total combined group turnover and associate turnover has been given as a memorandum item. • Share of associate operating result immediately after group operating result and share of joint venture operating result (if any), any amortisation or write-down of goodwill arising on acquiring the joint venture should be charged at this point and disclosed. • Share of any FRS 3.20 exceptional items or of interest should be shown separately from amounts relating to the group. • At or below the level of profit before tax, include the LLP's share of the relevant amount for associates within the amounts for the group and for items below this level disclose the amounts relating to associates.		

8 STATEMENT OF TOTAL RECOGNISED GAINS AND LOSSES (STRGL)

		Reference	Yes/no/na
8.1	Where there have been gains and losses in the period other than the profit or loss for the period, a statement of recognised gains and losses should be presented. This is a primary statement and should be presented with the same prominence as the other primary statements.	FRS 3.27	

		Reference	*Yes/no/na*
8.2	If no STRGL is being presented because there have been no gains and losses other than profit or loss for the period, then a statement of that fact should be made immediately below the profit and loss account.	FRS 3.57	
8.3	Where consolidated accounts are prepared, show separately for each heading the share of the joint ventures' or associates total recognised gains and losses either in the statement or in a note cross-referenced from the statement.		
8.4	Impairment losses recognised in the STRGL should be disclosed separately on the face of the STRGL.	FRS 11.67	

9 PRIOR PERIOD ADJUSTMENTS

		Reference	*Yes/no/na*
9.1	Disclose the particulars and reasons for each prior period adjustment.	Sch 4.4	
9.2	Restate the comparatives for the preceding period and adjust the opening balance of member's interests for the cumulative effect.	FRS 3.29	
9.3	Show the cumulative effect at the foot of the STRGL for the current period.	FRS 3.29	
9.4	Where practicable show the effect on the results of the prior period. Where this is not possible, state the reason.	FRS 3.29	

10 NOTE OF HISTORICAL COST PROFITS AND LOSSES

		Reference	*Yes/no/na*
10.1	A note of historical cost profits and losses is required only where there is a	FRS 3.26	

		Reference	*Yes/no/na*
	material difference between the result as disclosed in the profit and loss account and the result on an unmodified historical cost basis.		
10.2	Immediately following the profit and loss account or statement of total recognised gains and losses include a note which reconciles the reported profit/loss on ordinary activities before taxation to the equivalent historical cost amount and showing the profit or loss for the financial period available for division among members on an historical cost basis.	FRS 3.26	

11 PARENT LLP PROFIT AND LOSS ACCOUNT

		Reference	*Yes/no/na*
	Where the group accounts exclude the profit and loss account of the parent LLP, state that the exemption conferred by s 230 applies and give the parent LLP's profit or loss for the financial period available for division among members.		

12 BALANCE SHEET

		Reference	*Yes/no/na*
Fixed assets (generally)			
12.1	On the face of the balance sheet fixed assets must be analysed between: • Intangible assets. • Tangible assets. • Investments.	Sch 4	
12.2	Where assets are included at a valuation:	Sch 4.33	

		Reference	*Yes/no/na*
	• The items affected and basis of valuation of each such item. • The comparable historical cost amounts or the difference between historical cost amounts and balance sheet values (for cost and depreciation).		
12.3	In the accounting periods after an asset has suffered impairment: • For assets held at historical cost the impairment loss should be included within cumulative depreciation; the cost of the asset should not be reduced. • For revalued assets held at market value, the impairment loss should be included within the revalued carrying amount. • For revalued assets held at depreciated replacement cost, an impairment loss charged to the profit and loss account should be included within cumulative depreciation; the carrying amount of the asset should not be reduced and any loss charged to the STRGL should be deducted from the carrying amount.	FRS 11.68	
12.4	The discount rate used, where an impairment loss is measured by reference to value in use of a fixed asset or income generating unit. If a risk-free rate is used, some indication of the risk adjustments made to cash flows.	FRS 11.69	
12.5	Where an impairment loss recognised in a previous period is reversed in the current period, the reasons for the reversal and any changes in the assumptions upon which the calculation of recoverable amount is based.	FRS 11.70	

		Reference	*Yes/no/na*
12.6	Where an impairment loss would have been recognised in a previous period had the forecast future cash flows been more accurate, but the impairment has now reversed and the reversal of the loss is permitted to be recognised, disclose both the impairment and its subsequent reversal.	FRS 11.71	
12.7	Where, in measuring value in use, the projection period, before a steady or declining long-term growth rate has been assumed, extends to more than five years explain the length of the projection period and the reasons.	FRS 11.72	
Intangible assets – other than goodwill			
12.8	Analyse either on the face of the balance sheet or in the notes across the following headings: • Development costs. • Concessions, patents, licences, trademarks and similar rights and assets.	 Sch 4.F Sch 4.F	
Intangible assets – goodwill			
12.9	• Positive purchased goodwill. • Negative goodwill – should be shown separately immediately after positive goodwill. • Subtotal showing the net amount of positive and negative goodwill.	FRS 10.7, 48	
12.10	Separately for positive goodwill, negative goodwill and each class of capitalised intangible asset • Cost or revalued amount at the beginning of the period and at the balance sheet date. • Cumulative amount of provisions for amortisation or impairment at the beginning of the period and at the balance sheet date.	FRS 10.53, Sch 4.42	

		Reference	*Yes/no/na*
	• Separate disclosure of additions, disposals, revaluations and transfers. • Movements in provisions for amortisation and impairment, separately disclosing disposals, transfers, amortisation, impairment losses, reversals of past impairment losses and amounts of negative goodwill written back in the period. • The net carrying amount at the balance sheet date.		
12.11	Where the amortisation period or method has been changed following a review of the useful economic life, the reason and the effect should be disclosed if this is material.	FRS 10.56	
12.12	Where an intangible asset has been revalued state: • The year of the revaluation. • The amount of each valuation. • If the valuation was in the current year, the name and qualifications of the valuer.	FRS 10.61	
12.13	For revalued intangible assets disclose the original cost or fair value and the amount of any provision for amortisation that would have been provided based on that original cost or fair value.	FRS 10.61	
Tangible fixed assets			
12.14	Either on the face of the balance sheet or in the notes tangible fixed assets should be analysed across the following headings: • Land and buildings. • Plant and machinery. • Fixtures and fittings, tools and equipment.	Sch 4.F	

		Reference	*Yes/no/na*
	• Payments on account and assets under construction. • Other headings may be used where these are more appropriate to the nature of the LLP's business.		
12.15	Land and buildings should be further analysed between freehold, long leaseholds (those with not less than 50 years unexpired) and short leaseholds.	Sch 4.44	
12.16	Investment properties should be included at open market value.	SSAP 19.12	
12.17	For each class of fixed asset: • The aggregate cost or valuation at the beginning of the period and at the balance sheet date. • The movement in cost or valuation, analysed between additions, disposals, revaluations and transfers. • The accumulated provision for depreciation or impairment in value at the beginning of the period and at the balance sheet date. • The movement in the provision for depreciation or impairment, analysed between depreciation provisions made in the year, disposal, revaluation and transfers, impairment losses and reversals of past impairment losses and other adjustments. • The net book amount at the beginning of the period and at the balance sheet date.	Sch 4.42, FRS 15.100	
12.18	Where any class of tangible fixed assets have been revalued the following information should be disclosed for each class of asset in each reporting period:	FRS 15.74	

		Reference	*Yes/no/na*
	• The name and qualifications of the valuer(s) or the valuer's organisation and a description of its nature. • The basis or bases of valuation. • The date and amounts of the valuations. • Where historical cost records are available, the carrying amount that would have been included in the accounts had the tangible fixed assets been carried at historical cost less depreciation. • Whether the person(s) carrying out the valuation is (are) internal or external to the LLP. • Where the members are not aware of any material change in value and therefore the valuation(s) have not been updated, a statement to that effect. • Where the valuation has not been updated, or is not a full valuation, the date of the last full valuation.		
12.19	For revalued investment properties disclose: • The carrying value and investment revaluation reserve. • The names of the valuers or their qualifications, and where the valuer is a member or employee, a statement of that fact. • Bases of valuation (should be at open market value). • Changes in value should be shown as a movement on investment revaluation reserve, unless a deficit or its reversal on an individual property is expected to be permanent, in which case it is charged to the profit and loss account.	SSAP 19.15 SSSAP 19.12, Sch 4.43 SSAP 19.11 SSAP 19.13	

		Reference	*Yes/no/na*
	• Particulars of, reasons for and effect of failure to depreciate. True and fair override.		
12.20	Where finance costs are capitalised disclose: • The aggregate finance costs included in the cost of tangible fixed assets. • Finance costs capitalised during the period. • Finance costs recognised in the profit and loss account during the period. • The capitalisation rate used to determine the amount of finance costs capitalised during the period.	FRS 15.31	
12.21	For lessees, the gross amount and related accumulated depreciation of assets held under finance leases and hire purchase contracts by each major class of asset, or if combined with owned fixed assets, the net amount held under finance leases.	SSAP 21.49	
12.22	Where assets are leased to other parties under operating leases give the gross value of assets and related accumulated depreciation.	SSAP 21.59	
12.23	Website development costs may be capitalised in the following circumstances: • The expenditure is separately identifiable. • The technical feasibility and commercial viability of the website has been assessed with reasonable certainty. • The website will generate sales or revenues directly and the expenditure makes an enduring contribution to the revenue generating capabilities of the website.	UITF 29.12	

		Reference	*Yes/no/na*
	• There is a reasonable expectation that the present value of the future cash flows will be no less than the amounts capitalised. • Adequate resources exist, or are reasonably expected to be available, to enable the website project to be completed.		
Fixed asset investments			
12.24	On the face of the balance sheet or in the notes analyse separately: • Shares in group undertakings. • Loans to group undertakings. • Participating interests. • In group accounts, share of the net assets of associates including goodwill arising on the acquisition of associates (less any write-down or amortisation). The net amount of goodwill should be disclosed separately. • In group accounts, share of the net assets of its joint ventures including goodwill arising on the acquisition of joint ventures (less any write-down or amortisation). Disclose separately on the face of the balance sheet the LLP's share of gross assets and of liabilities of joint ventures. The net amount of goodwill should be disclosed separately. • Loans to undertakings in which the company has a participating interest. • Investments other than loans. • Other loans.	Sch 4.F FRS 9.29	
12.25	For each class of investment disclose: • The aggregate cost or valuation at the beginning of the period and at the balance sheet date.	Sch 4.42	

		Reference	*Yes/no/na*
	• The aggregate movement in cost or valuation, differentiating between additions, disposals, revaluations and transfers. • The aggregate accumulated provision for impairment in value at the beginning of the period and at the balance sheet date. • The aggregate movement in provisions, differentiating between provisions made in the year, disposal adjustments and other adjustments.		
12.26	Where fixed asset investments (other than listed investments) are stated at a valuation: • The year in which they were valued and the amounts. • In the case of assets valued during the financial year, the names of the persons who valued them, or their qualifications and the bases of valuation used.	Sch 4.43	
12.27	In respect of listed investments disclose: • The aggregate carrying amount. • The aggregate market value of those investments where it differs from the carrying amount.	Sch 4.45	
12.28	Where consolidated accounts are produced, state whether each subsidiary undertaking is included in the consolidation.	Sch 5.15(4)	
12.29	Where at the end of the year the LLP (group) held shares in a subsidiary, the group held shares in an associate, or the LLP (group) had other significant holdings (ie, exceeded 20 per cent or more of nominal value of any class of shares or the value exceeded 20 per cent of the investing LLP's (group's) assets), disclose the following:	Sch 5	

		Reference	*Yes/no/na*
	• Name of the undertaking. • Country of incorporation or, if unincorporated, the address of its principal place of business. • Identity and proportion of the nominal value of each class of shares held. • Shares held directly by the LLP and those held by subsidiary undertakings should be separately identified.		
12.30	The nature of the business of each principal subsidiary.	FRS 2.33	
12.31	Where group accounts are not prepared, for each material subsidiary and other significant holdings disclose the following: • The total of its capital and reserves at the end of its financial year. • Its profit or loss for that year. This information need not be given for: • Holdings of less than 50 per cent where the undertaking is not required to deliver and does not otherwise publish its balance sheet for the relevant financial year. • Holdings of 20 per cent or more (not being subsidiaries) if the LLP is exempt from producing group accounts by virtue of s 228 and the investment in such undertakings is disclosed in aggregate in the notes by way of the equity method of valuation. • Subsidiary undertakings if the reporting company is exempt from producing group accounts.	Sch 5	
12.32	Where a company has subsidiary undertakings and group accounts are not prepared:	Sch 5.1	

		Reference	*Yes/no/na*
	• State the reason. • State that the accounts present information about the LLP as an individual undertaking and not about its group.		
12.33	For each consolidated subsidiary included on a basis of information prepared to a different date or accounting period from that of the LLP, disclose: • The name of the subsidiary. • The accounting date or period of the subsidiary. • The reason for using the different date or period.	FRS 2.44	
12.34	If the LLP is a subsidiary undertaking, the name of the ultimate parent and, if known, its country of incorporation.	Sch 5.12	
12.35	If the LLP is a subsidiary undertaking, in respect of the parent which heads the largest group in which the LLP is a member and for which group accounts are prepared and also in respect of the parent of the smallest such group: • The name of the parent. • The country of incorporation and if it is unincorporated, the address of its principal place of business. • The addresses from which copies of the group accounts which are available to the public can be obtained.	Sch 5.11	
12.36	Where group accounts are required, for subsidiaries excluded from consolidation disclose the following: • The names of the subsidiaries excluded. • The reasons for exclusion from consolidation.	FRS 2.26	

		Reference	*Yes/no/na*
	• Particulars of balances between excluded subsidiaries and the rest of the group. • The nature and extent of transactions of the excluded subsidiaries with the rest of the group. • For an excluded subsidiary not equity accounted, any amounts included in the consolidated accounts in respect of dividends received and receivable from that subsidiary and any write-down in the period of the investment in and amounts due from that subsidiary.		
12.37	Where consolidated accounts are not prepared then, unless the LLP is exempt from preparing consolidated accounts, or would be if it had subsidiaries, show the following information by producing a separate set of accounts or by showing the relevant amounts, together with the effects of including them, as additional information to the LLP's own accounts: • As a separate fixed asset investment the investor's share of the net assets of its joint ventures or associates. • Goodwill arising on the acquisition of joint ventures or associates (less any write-down or amortisation) should be included in the carrying amount for joint ventures but disclosed separately. • Share of gross assets and liabilities of joint venture.	FRS 9.48	
Current assets			
12.38	Current assets should be stated at the lower of cost and net realisable value.	Sch 4.22	

		Reference	*Yes/no/na*
12.39	The total of current assets must be disclosed on the face of the balance sheet and it must be analysed across the following headings (either on the face of the balance sheet or in the notes to the accounts): • Stocks and work in progress. • Debtors. • Investments. • Cash at bank and in hand.	Sch 4	
Stocks, long-term contracts and revenue recognition			
12.40	Either on the face of the balance sheet or in the notes stocks should be analysed between: • Raw materials and consumables. • Work in progress. • Finished goods and goods for resale.	Sch 4.F	
12.41	Where the stated value of stock is materially different from replacement cost, disclose the difference.	Sch 4.26	
12.42	The components of long-term contracts should be disclosed as follows: • The excess of recorded revenue over payments received on account should be included within debtors as 'amounts recoverable on contracts'. • The excess of such payments after being matched with turnover and offset against long-term contract balances should be included within creditors as 'payments on account'. • The net costs of long-term contracts after transfers to cost of sales less foreseeable losses and payments on account not matched with turnover should be included	SSAP 9.30, UITF 40	

		Reference	*Yes/no/na*
	within stocks, as 'long-term contract balances', showing separately: • net cost less foreseeable losses; and • payments on account. • Any excess of provisions for foreseeable losses over costs incurred after transfers to cost of sale should be included within provisions for liabilities or creditors.		
Debtors			
12.43	Either on the face of the balance sheet or in the notes analyse debtors across the following headings: • Trade debtors. • Amounts owed by group undertakings. • Amounts owed by entities in which the LLP has a participating interest. • Amounts due from members. • Other debtors. • Prepayments and accrued income.	Sch 4.F SORP 60	
12.44	For each category of debtor show the amounts falling due after more than one year.	Sch 4.F(5)	
12.45	Where debtors due after more than one year are material in the context of total net current assets they should be disclosed on the face of the balance sheet.	UITF 4	
12.46	Where assets are leased to other parties under finance leases: • The net investment in finance leases and hire purchase contracts. • The cost of assets acquired for letting under finance leases.	SSAP 21.58	

		Reference	*Yes/no/na*
Current asset investments			
12.47	Either on the face of the balance sheet or in the notes current asset investments should be analysed between: • Shares in group undertakings. • Other investments.	Sch 4.F	
12.48	For listed current asset investments disclose: • The aggregate carrying amount. • The aggregate market value, if different.	Sch 4.45	
12.49	Groups containing limited companies only – net deferred tax assets should be disclosed as a separate subheading of debtors.	FRS 19.55	
Creditors – amounts due in less than one year			
12.50	The total of creditors due in less than one year must be disclosed on the face of the balance sheet and it must be analysed across the following headings (either on the face of the balance sheet or in the notes to the accounts): • Bank loans and overdrafts. • Obligations under finance leases. • Payments received on account. • Trade creditors. • Bills of exchange payable. • Amounts owed to group undertakings. • Amounts owed to undertakings in which the LLP has a participating interest. • Post retirement payments to former members*. • Other creditors, including taxation and social security (showing the amount for taxation and social security separately). • Accruals and deferred income.	Sch 4.F	

		Reference	*Yes/no/na*
12.51	Where the company has given security in respect of any debt included under each item shown under 'creditors' disclose: • The aggregate amount of any debt included under that item. • The nature of the security given.	Sch 4.48	
Net current assets			
12.52	Net of current assets and creditors due in less than one year to be shown on the face of the balance sheet.	Sch 4.F	
Total assets less current liabilities			
12.53	Total of fixed assets and net current assets to be shown on the face of the balance sheet.	Sch 4.F	
Creditors – amounts due in more than one year			
12.54	The total of creditors due in more than one year must be disclosed on the face of the balance sheet and it must be analysed across the following headings (either on the face of the balance sheet or in the notes to the accounts): • Bank loans and overdrafts. • Obligations under finance leases. • Payments received on account. • Trade creditors. • Bills of exchange payable. • Amounts owed to group undertakings. • Amounts owed to undertakings in which the LLP has a participating interest. • Post-retirement payments to former members*. • Other creditors, including taxation and social security (showing the amount for taxation and social security separately). • Accruals and deferred income.		

* Presentation dependent upon how entitlement is calculated.

		Reference	*Yes/no/na*
12.55	For each item in 'creditors' which falls due after more than one year disclose the aggregate of: • The amount of any instalments falling due after five years in respect of debts which are payable or repayable by instalments. • The amount of any debts not payable or repayable by instalments which fall due after five years.	Sch 4.48	
12.56	For each debt in which any amount is payable after five years, the payment terms and interest rate.	Sch 4.48	
12.57	Debt should be analysed between amounts falling due as shown below: • In one year or less or on demand. • In more than one year but not more than two years. • In more than two years but not more than five years. • In more than five years.	FRS 4.33	
Provisions for liabilities			
12.58	Either on the face of the balance sheet or in the notes disclose separately: • Post-retirement payments to former members*. • Deferred taxation. • Other provisions (giving particulars of any material provisions included in other provisions).	FRS 12	

* Presentation dependent upon how entitlement is calculated.

12.59	For each class of provision show: • The carrying amount at the start of the period. • The carrying amount at the end of the period.	FRS 12.89	

		Reference	*Yes/no/na*
	• Additional provisions made in the period including increases to existing provisions. • Amounts charged against the provision during the period. • Unused amounts reversed in the period. • Increase in the period in the discounted amount due to the passage of time and the effect of changes in the discount rate.		
12.60	For each class of provision give: • A brief description of the nature of the obligation and expected timing of any resulting transfers of economic benefit. • An indication of the uncertainties about the amount or timing of those transfers of economic benefits. • The amount of any expected reimbursement, stating the amount of any asset that has been recognised for that expected reimbursement.	FRS 12.90	
Deferred tax (groups only)			
12.61	• Total deferred tax balance (before discounting), showing the amount recognised for each significant type of timing difference separately. • Where applied, the impact of discounting on, and the discounted amount of, the deferred tax balance. • Movement between opening and closing net deferred tax balance analysed between: • amount charged or credited in the profit and loss account for the period;	FRS 19.61	

		Reference	*Yes/no/na*
	• amount charged or credited directly in the statement of recognised gains and losses for the period; and • movements arising from the acquisition or disposal of businesses.		
Net assets attributable to members of the LLP [excluding pension surplus/deficit]			
12.62	Where the LLP has a defined benefit pension scheme the amount of the surplus or deficit. Should be included at this place on the balance sheet.	SORP 51	
Net assets attributable to members of the LLP [including pension surplus/deficit]			
Loans and other debts due to members			
12.63	Loans and other debts due to members should be analysed between: • Loans and other debts due to members. • Members' capital classified as a liability under FRS 25. Separate disclosure is required of the following: • The aggregate amount of money advanced to members by way of loan. • The aggregate amount of money owed to members with respect of profits. • Where material, the amount relating to post-retirement benefits. • Other amounts.	SORP 48 SORP 59, 82 Sch 4	
12.64	Disclose separately amounts falling due after more than one year.	Sch 4 SORP 58	
12.65	• The notes to the accounts should explain where amounts included under this heading would rank in relation to other creditors who are unsecured in the event of a winding up.	SORP 56	

		Reference	*Yes/no/na*
	• Details of any protection afforded to creditors in the event of a winding up which is legally enforceable and cannot be revoked at will by the members should be included in the notes to the accounts. • Where no such protection is afforded, this should be noted.		
Minority interests			
12.66	In consolidated accounts minority interests should either be shown at this position or after members' other interests.	Sch 4A	
Members' other interests			
12.67	On the face of the balance sheet members' other interests classified as equity should be analysed between: • Members' capital. • Revaluation reserve. • Other reserves. Any unallocated profits should be included within other reserves. Where the LLP has made a loss and this is not allocated to the members, it should be deducted from other reserves.	SORP 48 SORP 54	
Total members' interests			
12.68	On the face of the balance sheet include as a memorandum item the following: • Loans and other debts due to members. • Members' other interests. • Amounts due from members.	SORP 51	
Approval of accounts			
12.69	A statement that the financial statements were approved by the members together with the date of approval and the signature and name of the designated member(s) authorised to sign the accounts.		

13 RECONCILIATION OF MEMBERS' INTERESTS

		Reference	*Yes/No/na*
Reconciliation of members' interests			
13.1	A table should be presented showing all movements in members' interests. This should be analysed, as a minimum, across the following headings: (a) Members' capital classified as equity. (b) Revaluation reserve. (c) Other reserves. (d) Total of (a) to (c). (e) Loans and other debts due to members less any amounts due from members included in debtors. (f) Total of (d) and (e).	SORP 53	
Amounts at the beginning of the period			
13.2	The following should be disclosed with respect to amounts at the beginning of the period: • Amounts due to members. • Amounts due from members. • The balances of members' interests.	SORP 53	
Profit for the period			
13.3	Disclose separately: • Members' remuneration charged as an expense, including employment and retirement benefit costs. • The profit or loss available for discretionary division among members.	SORP 53	
Members' interests after profit/loss for the period			
13.4	Members' interests after profit/loss for the period.	SORP 53	

		Reference	*Yes/No/na*
Movements in members' interests			
13.5	The following should be shown separately: • Other divisions of profits or losses. • Surplus on revaluation of fixed assets. • Capital introduced by members. • Repayments of capital. • Repayments of debt (including members' capital classified as a liability). • Drawings. • Other movements (explained where these are significant). • In group accounts the exchange differences arising on the re-translation of the investment in foreign subsidiaries.	SORP 53	
Closing balances			
13.6	Show separately the following amounts at the period end: • Amounts due to members. • Amounts due from members. • The balance of members' interests.	SORP 53	

14 CASH FLOW STATEMENT

		Reference	*Yes/No/na*
Cash flow headings			
14.1	The cash flow statement should include the following headings: • Operating activities. • Dividends from joint ventures and associates (consolidated accounts only).	FRS 1	

		Reference	*Yes/No/na*
	• Returns on investments and servicing of finance. • Taxation (consolidated accounts only). • Capital expenditure and financial investment. • Acquisitions and disposals. • Transactions with members and former members. • Management of liquid resources. • Financing.		
Operating cash flows			
14.2	A reconciliation between operating profit or loss reported in the profit and loss account and the net cash flow from operating activities, showing separately movements in stocks or work in progress, debtors and creditors related to operating activities and other differences between cash flow and profits (eg depreciation and impairment).	FRS 1.12	
Returns on investments and servicing of finance			
14.3	Show the following separately: • Interest received. • Dividends received. • Interest paid. • Interest element of finance lease rental payments.	 FRS 1.14 FRS 1.14 FRS 1.15 FRS 1.15	
Taxation			
14.4	Show the following separately: • UK tax paid. • Foreign tax paid	FRS 1.16	
Capital expenditure and financial investment			
14.5	Show separately: • Purchase of property plant and equipment.	 FRS 1.20	

		Reference	*Yes/No/na*
	• Sale of property, plant or equipment. • Purchase of investments.	FRS 1.20 FRS 1.21	
Acquisitions and disposals			
14.6	Show separately: • Sale of investments in subsidiary undertakings. • Sale of investments in associates or joint ventures. • Sale of trades or businesses. • Purchase of investments in subsidiary undertakings. • Net cash acquired with subsidiary undertakings. • Purchase of investments in associates or joint ventures. • Purchase of trades or businesses.	FRS 1.23, 1.24	
14.7	Where the group has acquired or disposed of a subsidiary, a summary of the effects of the acquisition or disposal, indicating how much of the consideration comprised cash, and the amounts of cash transferred.	FRS 1.45	
14.8	The material effects on amounts reported under each standard heading of cash flows in respect of a subsidiary acquired or disposed of in the period.	FRS 1.45	
Transactions with members and former members			
14.9	As a minimum the following should be analysed: • Payments to members. • Contributions by members. • Retirement benefits paid to former members.	SORP 67	
Liquid resources			
14.10	Explain what is included in 'liquid resources'.	FRS 1.26	

		Reference	*Yes/No/na*
14.11	Cash flow movements should be analysed across the following: • Withdrawals from short-term deposits. • Inflows from disposals or redemption of any other investments held as liquid resources. • Payments into short-term deposits. • Payments into any other investments held as liquid resources.	FRS 1.27, 1.28	
Financing			
14.12	Disclose at least the following: • Receipts from issuing loans and other long-term and short-term borrowings. • Repayments of amounts borrowed. • The capital element of finance lease rental payments. • Financing cash flows received from or paid to equity accounted entities.	FRS 1.30 FRS 1.30 FRS 1.31 FRS 1.32	
Movement in net debt			
14.13	A reconciliation between the movement in cash and the movement in net debt. The changes in net debt should be analysed from the opening to the closing balances showing separately: • Cash flows. • Acquisitions and disposals of subsidiaries. • Other non-cash changes. • Changes in market value and exchange rate movements.	FRS 1.33	
Non-cash transactions			
14.14	Material non-cash transactions where disclosure is necessary for an understanding of the underlying transactions.	FRS 1.46	

15 ACCOUNTING POLICIES

		Reference	*Yes/no/na*
General			
15.1	The accounting policies used for dealing with items which are judged to be material should be explained in the accounts.	FRS 18.55	
15.2	State that the accounts have been prepared in accordance with applicable accounting standards and the SORP.	Sch 4.36, SORP 93	
15.3	If accounts are prepared on the basis of presumptions which differ from any of the accounting principles give: • Particulars of the departure. • The reasons for the departure. • The effects.	Sch 4.15	
15.4	Give an explanation of significant estimation techniques adopted.	FRS 18.55	
15.5	Give details of any changes to the accounting policies from those used in the previous period, including: • A brief explanation of why the new policy is thought more appropriate. • Where practicable, the effect of a prior period adjustment on the results of the preceding period. • Where practicable, an indication of the effect of the change on the results of the current year.	FRS 18.55	
15.6	Where the effect of a change to an estimation technique is material, give a description of: • The change. • Where practicable, the effect of the change on the results for the current period.	FRS 18.55	

		Reference	*Yes/no/na*
Members' remuneration and members' interest			
15.7	Explain the basis on which each element of members' remuneration (ie members' remuneration charged as an expense or retained profit or loss available for discretionary division among members) has been determined.	SORP 45	
Revenue recognition and turnover			
15.8	• Disclose the policies adopted for recognising revenue. • Disclose that turnover is the amount derived from ordinary activities, and stated after discounts and net of VAT.	FRS 5 ANG, UITF 40 s 262	
Government grants			
15.9	Disclose the accounting policy adopted for government grants.	SSAP 4.28	
Stocks and long-term contracts			
15.10	State the accounting policy applied to stocks and long-term contracts.	SSAP 9.32	
Intangible fixed assets			
15.11	The reasons for capitalising development costs and the period of write off.	Sch 4.20	
15.12	Basis of any valuation.		
15.13	The methods of amortisation of goodwill and intangible assets. • The periods of amortisation. • The reason for choosing those periods. • Where either the amortisation period or method have been changed in the year, the reason for and effect, if material, of the change. • The reasons for rebutting the 20-year presumption where goodwill		

		Reference	*Yes/no/na*
	or an intangible asset is amortised over a period exceeding 20 years from the date of acquisition or is not amortised.		
15.14	Where goodwill is not amortised: • The accounts should state that they depart from the specific requirement of the LLPA to amortise goodwill over a finite period for the overriding purpose of giving a true and fair view. • An estimate of the financial effect of taking advantage of the true and fair override.	FRS 10.59	
15.15	Period over which negative goodwill is being written back in the profit and loss account.	FRS 10.63	
Capitalisation of finance costs			
15.16	Where a policy of capitalising finance costs is adopted disclose the assets affected and the basis of allocation of the finance cost.	FRS 15.31	
Development costs			
15.17	Where development costs are capitalised, the reasons for capitalisation and the write off period.	SSAP 13.30	
Foreign currency			
15.18	State the following: • The method for translating accounts of foreign enterprises. • The treatment of foreign exchange differences.	SSAP 20.59	
Leases			
15.19	Disclose the policies for the treatment of operating and finance leases together with accounting for lease incentives.	SSAP 21.57	

		Reference	*Yes/no/na*
Going concern			

15.20	Disclose:
	• Any material uncertainties related to events or conditions that may cast doubt on the ability of the LLP to continue as a going concern.
	• Where the foreseeable future considered by the members has been limited to a period of less than one year from the approval of the accounts, that fact should be disclosed.
	• Where the accounts are not prepared on a going concern basis:
	  • that fact;
	  • the basis on which the accounts are prepared;
	  • the reason why the LLP is not considered to be a going concern.
		FRS 18.61	

Post-retirement payments to members			
15.21	The policy in respect of post-retirement payments to members.	SORP 85	
Basis of consolidation			
15.22	Disclosure should include the treatment of subsidiaries acquired or sold in the period and the method of accounting (acquisition or merger) adopted.		
Tangible fixed assets			
15.23	Disclosure should include: • The depreciation methods used. • The useful economic lives or depreciation rates used.	FRS 15.100	
Associates			
15.24	Accounting treatment applied.		

		Reference	*Yes/no/na*
Taxation			
15.25	Where the LLP has subsidiaries disclose the basis of both the current and deferred tax charges and provisions.		

16 RETIREMENT BENEFITS

		Reference	*Yes/no/na*
Defined contribution schemes			
16.1	The nature of the scheme, the cost for the period and any outstanding or pre-paid contributions at the balance sheet date.	FRS 17.75	
Defined benefit schemes*			
16.2	A general description of the type of scheme.	FRS 17.77	
16.3	A reconciliation of opening and closing balances of the present value of scheme liabilities showing separately, if applicable, the effects during the period attributable to each of the following: • current service cost; • interest cost; • contributions by scheme participants; • actuarial gains and losses; • foreign currency exchange rate changes on schemes measured in a currency different from the LLP's presentation currency; • benefits paid; • past service cost; • business combinations; • curtailments; and • settlements.	FRS 17.77	

		Reference	*Yes/no/na*
16.4	An analysis of scheme liabilities into amounts arising from schemes that are wholly unfunded and amounts arising from schemes that are wholly or partly funded.	FRS 17.77	
16.5	A reconciliation of the opening and closing balances of the fair value of scheme assets showing separately, if applicable, the effects during the period attributable to each of the following: • expected rate of return on scheme assets; • actuarial gains and losses; • foreign currency exchange rate changes on schemes measured in a currency different from the LLP's presentation currency; • contributions by the employer; • contributions by scheme participants; • benefits paid; • business combinations; and • settlements.	FRS 17.77	
16.6	A reconciliation of the present value of scheme liabilities and the fair value of the scheme assets to the assets and liabilities recognised in the balance sheet, showing at least: • any past service cost not recognised in the balance sheet; • any amount not recognised as an asset; and • any other amounts recognised in the balance sheet.	FRS 17.77	
16.7	The total expense recognised in profit or loss for each of the following, and the line item(s) in which they are included: • current service cost;	FRS 17.77	

		Reference	*Yes/no/na*
	• interest cost; • expected return on scheme assets; • past service cost; • the effect of any curtailment or settlement; and • the effect of the limit in the ability to recognise an asset.		
16.8	The total amounts recognised in the statement of total recognised gains and losses for each of the following: • actuarial gains and losses; and • the effect of the limit in the ability to recognise an asset.	FRS 17.77	
16.9	The cumulative amount of actuarial gains and losses recognised in the statement of total recognised gains and losses.	FRS 17.77	
16.10	For each major category of scheme assets, including, but not limited to, equity instruments, debt instruments, property, and all other assets, the percentage or amount that each major category constitutes of the fair value of the total scheme assets.	FRS 17.77	
16.11	A narrative description of the basis used to determine the overall expected rate of return on assets, including the effect of the major categories of scheme assets.	FRS 17.77	
16.12	The actual return on scheme assets.	FRS 17.77	
16.13	The principal actuarial assumptions used as at the balance sheet date, including, where applicable: • the discount rates; • the expected rates of return on any assets of the scheme for the periods presented in the financial statements;	FRS 17.77	

		Reference	*Yes/no/na*
	• the expected rates of salary increases (and of changes in an index or other variable specified in the formal or constructive terms of a scheme as the basis for future benefit increases); • retirement healthcare cost trend rates; and • any other material actuarial assumptions used. Disclosure of each actuarial assumption should be in absolute terms (for example, as an absolute percentage) and not just as a margin between different percentages or other variables.		
16.14	The effect of an increase of one percentage point and the effect of a decrease of one percentage point in the assumed retirement healthcare cost trend rates on: • the aggregate of the current service cost and interest cost components of net periodic retirement healthcare costs; and • the accumulated retirement healthcare obligation for healthcare costs.	FRS 17.77	
16.15	The amounts for the current accounting period and previous four accounting periods of: • the present value of the scheme liabilities, the fair value of the scheme assets and the surplus or deficit in the scheme; and • the experience adjustments arising on: • the scheme liabilities expressed either as (1) an amount or (2) a percentage of the scheme liabilities at the balance sheet date; and	FRS 17.77	

		Reference	*Yes/no/na*
	• the assets of the scheme expressed either as (1) an amount or (2) a percentage of the assets of the scheme at the balance sheet date.		
16.16	The employer's best estimate, as soon as it can reasonably be determined, of contributions expected to be paid to the scheme during the accounting period beginning after the balance sheet date.	FRS 17.77	
Retirement benefits of members			
16.17	Amounts recognised in respect of current members should be included within members' remuneration charged as an expense.	SORP 81	
16.18	Changes in the liability in respect of former members should be expensed in the relevant expense item in the profit and loss account and should not be included within members' remuneration charged as an expense.	SORP 81	
16.19	Liabilities in respect of former members should be included either within Provisions for Liabilities or Creditors.	SORP 82	
16.20	Liabilities in respect of current members should be shown separately, if material, as a component of 'Loans and other debts due to members'.	SORP 82	
16.21	Where the liability has been discounted, the unwinding of the discount should be presented next to the interest cost line in the profit and loss accounts to the extent that it relates to former members. Where it relates to current members it should be included in 'Members' remuneration charged as an expense'.	SORP 83	

* Reflects the amendments to FRS 17 applying to periods beginning on or after 1 January 2007.

17 OTHER DISCLOSURES

		Reference	*Yes/no/na*
Contingencies and commitments			
17.1	For each class of contingent liability disclose: • A brief description of the nature of the contingent liability. • An estimate of its financial effect. • An indication of the uncertainties relating to the amount or timing of any outflow. • Whether any valuable security has been given for the liability, and if so, details of the security. • The possibility of any reimbursement.	FRS 12.91	
17.2	For any contingent gain disclose: • A brief description of the nature of the contingency. • An estimate of its financial effect.	FRS 12.94	
17.3	Where some or all of the disclosures in respect of provisions, contingent liabilities or contingent assets are not given because to do so would be seriously prejudicial to the position of the LLP in relation to the matter, disclose: • The general nature of the dispute. • The fact that, and reason why, the information has not been disclosed.	FRS 12.97	
17.4	Where the LLP has entered into any guarantee or indemnity with respect to the borrowings of a member or members personally, where material this should be disclosed in the accounts.	SORP 117	
17.5	Particulars of any charge on the LLP's assets to secure the liabilities of any other person, including, where practicable, the amount secured.	Sch 4.50	

		Reference	*Yes/no/na*
17.6	The total amount of capital expenditures contracted for but not provided for in the accounts.	Sch 4.50	
17.7	Other financial commitments which have not been provided for and are relevant to assessing the LLP's state of affairs.	Sch 4.50	
17.8	Disclose separately guarantees and other financial commitments undertaken on behalf of or for the benefit of: • The parent company and fellow subsidiary undertakings. • Subsidiary undertakings. • Other parties.	Sch 4.59	
17.9	Lease payments which the lessee is committed to make during the next year under non-cancellable operating leases, analysed between those which expire: • Within one year. • Within two to five years inclusive. • Over five years from the balance sheet date. Show separately those in respect of land and buildings and other operating leases.	SSAP 21.56	
17.10	Any commitments entered into at the balance sheet date in respect of finance leases which start after the year end.	SSAP 21.54	
Segment information			
17.11	Where the LLP carries on substantially different classes of business or supplies substantially different geographical markets disclose turnover for each class of business and geographical market by destination.	Sch 4.55	

		Reference	*Yes/no/na*
17.12	Where the provisions of SSAP 25 apply: • Turnover derived from external customers and turnover derived from other segments for each class of business and geographical market by origin. • Segment result before taxation, minority interest and extraordinary items for each class of business and geographical segment. • Net assets by class of business and geographical segment.	SSAP 25.34	
Business combinations			
17.13	For each business combination made in the year disclose: • The names of the combining entities. • The name of acquired undertaking. • Whether the acquisition has been accounted for by the acquisition or merger method. • The date of combination.	FRS 6.21	

17.14	For each material acquisition and other acquisitions in aggregate disclose:
	• A table showing for each class of acquired assets and liabilities:
	    • Book values immediately before acquisition.
	    • Fair value adjustments (analysed between revaluations, adjustments to achieve consistency of accounting policies and other significant adjustments).
	    • The reasons for the fair value adjustments.
		FRS 6.25	

		Reference	Yes/no/na
	• Fair values at the date of acquisition. • The amount of purchased goodwill or negative goodwill arising on the acquisition. • Where the fair values of the assets, liabilities or consideration are on a provisional basis this fact and the reasons should be stated. • Subsequent material adjustments to provisional values, with corresponding adjustments to goodwill should be disclosed and explained. • Composition and fair value of consideration. • Nature of deferred or contingent purchase consideration. • Where there is contingent consideration, give the range of possible outcomes and principal factors affecting outcome.		
17.15	For each material acquisition, profit after tax and minority interest of the acquired entity for the period from the beginning of its financial period to the date of acquisition, giving the date its financial period began, and for its previous financial period.	FRS 6.35	
17.16	For each substantial acquisition include in the notes to the accounts: • A summarised profit and loss account and statement of total recognised gains and losses for the period from the beginning of its financial period to the effective date of acquisition, giving the date its financial period began. • Profit after tax and minority interest for the acquired entity's previous financial period and the date on which that period began.	FRS 6.36	

		Reference	*Yes/no/na*
Related parties and controlling party			
17.17	Where the LLP is controlled by another party, the name of that party should be disclosed.	FRS 8.5	
17.18	Where there have been material transactions between the LLP and a related party, the following should be disclosed: • the name of the related parties; • a description of the relationship between the parties; • a description of the transactions; • the amounts involved; • any other elements of the transactions necessary for an understanding of the financial statements; • the amounts due to or from the related parties at the balance sheet date and provisions for doubtful debts due from such parties at that date; • amounts written off in the period in respect of debts due to or from related parties.	FRS 8.6	
Subsequent events			
17.19	Any non-adjusting post balance sheet events whose disclosure is necessary for the accounts to give a true and fair view.	FRS 21.21	

Index

[all references are to paragraph number]